TRAVEL PUZZLES for Clever Kids

Puzzles and solutions
by Dr Gareth Moore
B.Sc (Hons) M.Phil Ph.D

Illustrations and cover
artwork by Chris Dickason

Designed by Zoe Bradley

☆

Edited by Joe Fullman and Frances Evans

☆

Cover Design by Angie Allison

TRAVEL PUZZLES for Clever Kids

Buster Books

First published in Great Britain in 2019 by Buster Books,
an imprint of Michael O'Mara Books Limited,
9 Lion Yard, Tremadoc Road, London SW4 7NQ

www.mombooks.com/buster

Buster Books

@BusterBooks

@Buster_Books

Puzzles and solutions © Gareth Moore 2019

Illustrations and layouts © Buster Books 2019

A CIP catalogue record for this book is available from the British Library.

ISBN: 978-1-78055-563-8

4 6 8 10 9 7 5 3

Papers used by Buster Books are natural, recyclable products made of wood from
well-managed, FSC®-certified forests and other controlled sources. The manufacturing
processes conform to the environmental regulations of the country of origin.

Printed and bound in February 2021 by CPI Group (UK) Ltd,
108 Beddington Lane, Croydon, CR0 4YY, United Kingdom

MIX
Paper from
responsible sources
FSC® C020471

INTRODUCTION

Get ready to go on a fun-filled journey with this exciting book that's packed full of puzzles. Travel through over 100 puzzles, all designed to make any trip much more fun. Each puzzle can be tackled on its own and you can work through the book at your own pace.

At the top of every page, there is a space for you to write how much time it took you to complete the puzzle. Don't be afraid to make notes on the pages – this can be a good tactic to help you keep track of your thoughts. There are some blank pages at the back of the book that you can use for working out your answers, too.

Read the simple instructions on each page before tackling a puzzle. If you get stuck, read the instructions again in case there's something you missed. Work in pencil so you can rub things out and have another try.

If you are still stuck, you could also try asking an adult, although did you know that your brain is actually much more powerful than a grown-up's? When you get older, your brain gets rid of lots of bits of information it thinks it doesn't need any more. That means you might be better at solving these puzzles than older people are.

If you're **REALLY** stuck, have a peek at the answers at the back of the book, and then try to work out how you could have got to that solution yourself.

Now, good luck and have fun!

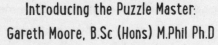

Introducing the Puzzle Master:
Gareth Moore, B.Sc (Hons) M.Phil Ph.D

Dr Gareth Moore is an Ace Puzzler, and author of lots of puzzle and brain-training books.

He created an online brain-training site called BrainedUp.com, and runs an online puzzle site called PuzzleMix.com. Gareth has a Ph.D from the University of Cambridge, where he taught machines to understand spoken English.

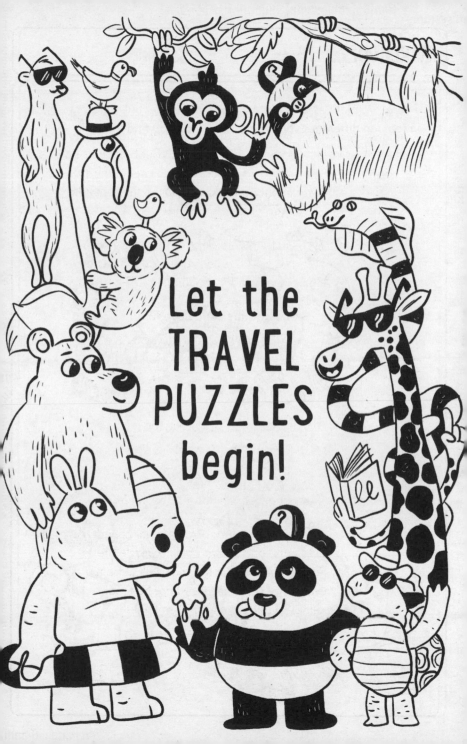

Let the
TRAVEL
PUZZLES
begin!

These two pictures look identical at first glance, but there are in fact ten differences between them. Can you find them all?

Can you help these sailors solve the number pyramids on their sails? Each square should contain a number that is equal to the sum of the two blocks immediately beneath it.

a)

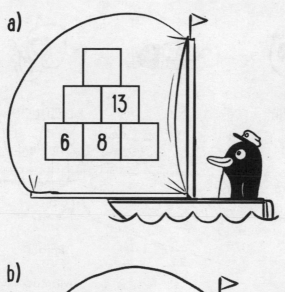

b)

Using your knowledge of the world, can you draw lines to join each country to its capital city? One is already done to show you how it works.

COUNTRY	CAPITAL CITY
Argentina	Canberra
Australia	Buenos Aires
Canada	New Delhi
China	Nairobi
India	Moscow
Kenya	Beijing
Russia	Ottawa

Solve these mini sudoku puzzles by placing a number from 1 to 4 in each empty square. Once complete, every row, column and bold-lined 2x2 box must contain each number from 1 to 4.

a)

			3
1			
			4
3			

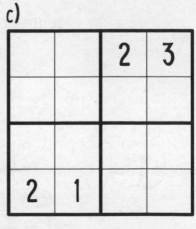

b)

		1	
		4	
	4		
	2		

c)

		2	3
2	1		

Can you crack the cunning code below? Shift each letter backwards by one letter in the alphabet to reveal an amazing fact about the Earth. Here's the alphabet to help you:

A B C D E F G H I J K L M N O P Q R S T U V W X Y Z

For example, you should change B to A, C to B, D to C, and so on. But don't change any of the punctuation or numbers.

UIF IPUUFTU QMBDF PO FBSUI JT EFBU

....

WBMMFZ JO UIF VOJUFE TUBUFT. BO BJS

....

UFNQFSBUVSF PG 56.7°D (134°G) XBT PODF

....

SFDPSEFE UIFSF!

....

Imagine cutting out and folding up the image at the top of the page in order to make a cube. Which one of the four images at the bottom of the page would match that cube? A good way to tackle this puzzle is to first work out which cubes are clearly wrong. The remaining cube must be the correct one.

If you get stuck, you could draw a copy of the image, cut it out and fold it up.

a)

b)

c)

d)

TIME ....

How many words can you find in this word square? Start on any letter, then move in any direction (including diagonally) to a touching letter. Keep moving to touching letters until you have spelled out a word of three or more letters. Don't visit any square more than once within the word. Can you find the one word that uses all of the letters?

EASY TARGET: 10 words
MEDIUM TARGET: 20 words
HARD TARGET: 30 words

R	I	A
E	T	N
S	L	G

Join the dots to reveal an exotic creature! Start at 1 and draw a straight line to 2, then another straight line to 3 and so on, until you reach dot 51. What have you drawn?

Can you help this family of mice get to their plane on time by finding a path through this airport maze?

In the puzzles below, can you draw a single loop that passes through the centre of every white square, using only horizontal and vertical lines? The loop cannot cross over itself or pass through a black square, or visit any square more than once.

Here's an example solution. Notice how the line passes through the centre of every white square:

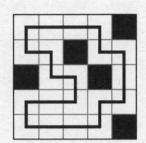

a)

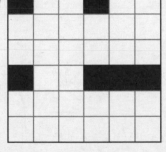

b)

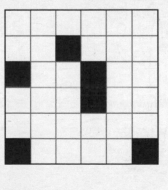

This snap-happy tourist is travelling from the USA to the United Kingdom for a holiday. Before she leaves, she wants to change some of her US dollars into UK pounds.

At the time that she travels, the exchange rate is 3 to 2, meaning that for every 3 US dollars she can get 2 UK pounds.

1) If she has 6 US dollars in her bag, how many UK pounds is this worth?

Answer: .....4.....................

2) If she has 20 UK pounds left at the end of her trip, how many US dollars is this worth?

Answer: ....

Can you find all of these beach-themed words in the grid below? They may be written in any direction: forwards, backwards, up, down or diagonally.

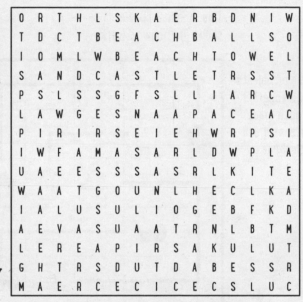

```
O R T H L S K A E R B D N I W
T D C T B E A C H B A L L S O
I O M L W B E A C H T O W E L
S A N D C A S T L E T R S S T
P S L S S G F S L L I A R C W
L A W G E S N A A P A C E A C
P I R I R S E I E H W R P S I
I W F A M A S A R L D W P L A
U A E E S S A S R L K I T E
W A A T G O U N L H E C L K A
I A L U S U L I O G E B F K D
A E V A S U A A T R N L B T M
L E R E A P I R S A K U L U T
G H T R S D U T D A B E S S R
M A E R C E C I C E C S L U C
```

BEACH BALL	PARASOL	SUNGLASSES
BEACH TOWEL	RUBBER RING	SWIMSUIT
FLIPPERS	SANDCASTLE	WAVES
ICE CREAM	SEASHELLS	WETSUIT
KITE	SNORKEL	WINDBREAK
LIFEGUARD		

Can you draw paths to connect each pair of identical objects together? The paths must be made up of only horizontal and vertical lines, and can't cross or touch each other. No more than one path can enter any grid square.

This finished puzzle shows you how it works:

Each pair of objects is linked together by a path made of horizontal and vertical lines.

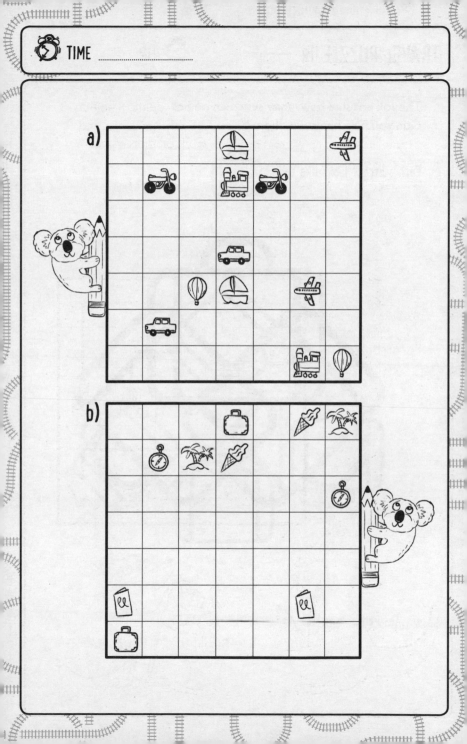

This fox isn't sure how many suitcases he has.
Can you help him count them?

Each suitcase looks like this:

Answer: ....

Alex, Beth and Catherine are building sandcastles on the beach. Their sandcastles are three different sizes. One of the sandcastles is decorated with just shells, one is decorated with just stones and one is just plain sand.

You also know the following:

- Beth's castle is bigger than Catherine's.

- Catherine's castle does not have stones on it.

- The castle with shells on it is the smallest.

- Catherine's castle is not the smallest.

Can you work out who built the biggest castle and who built the smallest castle? Also, can you work out which two castles were decorated and in what way?

Alex's castle is .... and has ....

Beth's castle is .... and has ....

Catherine's castle is .... and has ....

Can you help these animals work out which number should come next in each of the sequences?

The first sequence has been done for you as an example. The final number – after 13, 15, 17, 19, 21, 23 – is 25 because the sequence is 'add 2 at each step'. But what are the other sequences?

a)

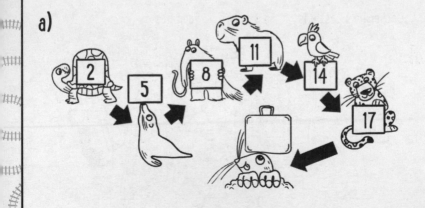

b)

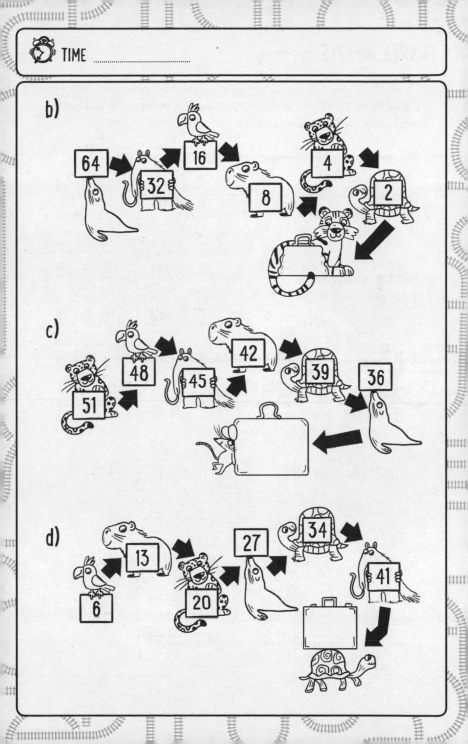

64 → 32 → 16 → 8 → 4 → 2

c)

51 → 48 → 45 → 42 → 39 → 36

d)

6 → 13 → 20 → 27 → 34 → 41

TRAVEL PUZZLE 17 →

Solve these futoshiki puzzles by placing the numbers 1 to 4 once each into every row and column.

You must obey the 'greater than' signs. These are arrows that always point from the bigger number to the smaller number of a pair. For example, you could have '3 > 1' because 3 is greater than 1. However, '1 > 2' would be wrong because 1 is not greater in value than 2.

Here's a finished puzzle to show you how it works:

4	1	2 <	3
∨		∨	
3	2	1	4
1	3	4	2
∧		∨	
2 <	4	3	1

a)

1			3
∧		∧	
	1		
			∨
>		1	
∨			
3		>	1

b)

	<		3
		1	^
	^		
	3		
2	<	v	>

c)

	3		
		^	< 4
^			
2			
	<	1	< v

The letters in each of the words below have been scrambled up. Can you rearrange each set of letters to spell something you might take on holiday with you? For example, ACDR could be rearranged to spell CARD.

a) AHT

b) BKOO

c) AACEMR

d) AOPPRSST

e) ACEISSTU

Fancy a game of number darts? To play, you'll need to form each of the target sums below by choosing one number from each ring of the dartboard and then adding them both together.

For example, you could form a sum of 12 by picking 3 from the innermost ring and 9 from the outermost ring. You can reuse numbers to make different target sums.

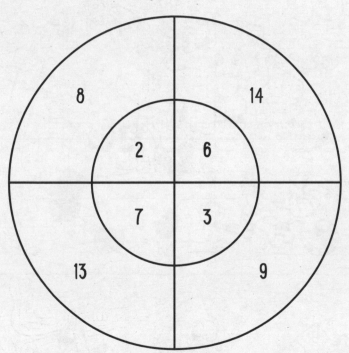

TARGET SUMS:

14 = ...

17 = ...

19 = ...

Oh no! One of the pieces is missing from this jigsaw puzzle and now you can't complete it. By working out where the remaining pieces below will fit, can you work out which piece is missing?

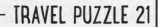
Can you fill in the empty squares so that each grid contains
every number from 1 to 16 once each?

THE RULES

- You must be able to start at '1' and then move to '2', '3', '4'
  and so on, moving only to touching grid squares.

- You can move left, right, up or down between squares,
  but not diagonally.

This finished puzzle
shows you how it works:

10	9	8	1
11	12	7	2
16	13	6	3
15	14	5	4

a)

13			4
	11	6	
	10	7	
16			1

b)

16			11
5			8

⏰ TIME ....

Can you help the alligators find their way through this circular-shaped hotel maze to get to the swimming pool?

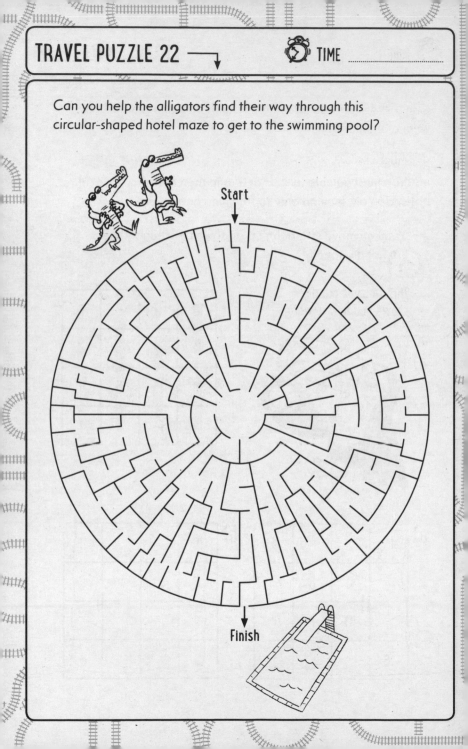

Start

Finish

Can you solve these three brain chains in your head, without writing anything down?

Start with the value at the top of each tree. Do what the maths instructions say in turn until you reach the empty box at the bottom. Write your answer in there.

a) 7

+ 16

- 20

+ 9

x 2

- 11

= ....

b) 6

+ 1

x 5

x 2

÷ 7

x 2

= ....

c) 9

÷ 3

+ 11

- 4

+ 2

x 4

= ....

TIME ....

Can you fit all of the geography-themed words into this crossword grid, placing each word either horizontally or vertically?

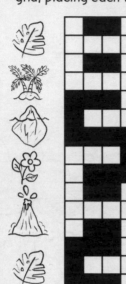

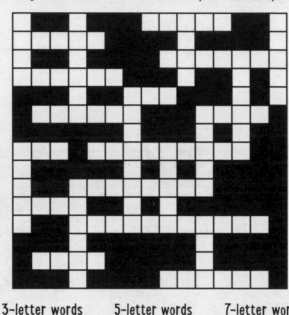

3-letter words
BAY
SEA

4-letter words
CAVE
LAKE
PEAK
POND
VELD
WOOD

5-letter words
BEACH
GORGE
OCEAN
PLAIN
RIVER
SWAMP

6-letter words
CAVERN
DESERT
ISLAND
MEADOW
STEPPE
TUNDRA

7-letter word
GLACIER

8-letter words
MOUNTAIN
SAVANNAH

9-letter word
GRASSLAND

11-letter word
ARCHIPELAGO

This safari park has three different types of animal in it — rhinos, elephants and ostriches.

Can you draw three straight lines to divide the park into four areas, so that each area contains exactly one of each type of animal?

Solve these odd-even sudoku puzzles by placing a number from 1 to 6 in each empty square. Once complete, every row, column and bold-lined 3x2 box must contain each number from 1 to 6. Shaded squares must contain even numbers (2, 4, 6) and unshaded squares must contain odd numbers (1, 3, 5).

a)

b)

		3	1	2	6	
	4				1	
	6				3	
	1	6	5	2		

TRAVEL PUZZLE 27 →

 TIME ....

Using your knowledge of the world, can you draw lines to join each country to one of its best-known tourist attractions? One is already done for you to show you how it works.

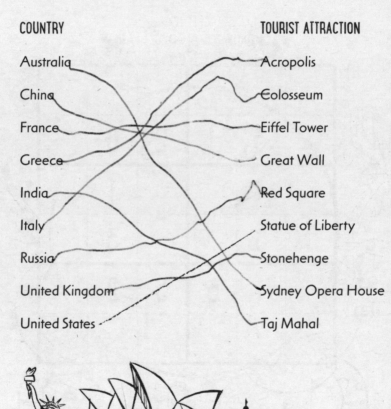

COUNTRY	TOURIST ATTRACTION
Australia	Acropolis
China	Colosseum
France	Eiffel Tower
Greece	Great Wall
India	Red Square
Italy	Statue of Liberty
Russia	Stonehenge
United Kingdom	Sydney Opera House
United States	Taj Mahal

How many words can you find in this word circle? Each word must use the centre letter plus two or more other letters, in any order. However, you can't use a letter more times than it appears in the circle. Can you find the one word that uses all the letters?

EASY TARGET: 10 words
MEDIUM TARGET: 15 words
HARD TARGET: 20 words

Draw horizontal and vertical lines to join pairs of circles so that each pair contains one white circle and one shaded circle.

THE RULES

- Lines cannot cross over each other or cross over circles.

- Every circle must form part of one pair only.

Here is an example to show you how it works:

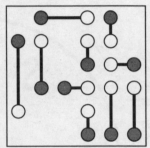

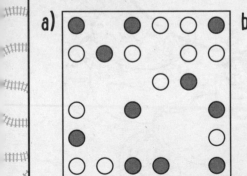

a)

b)

All of these lions look identical but, if you study them closely, you'll see that there are some subtle differences. Can you find the three matching pairs and draw lines to connect them?

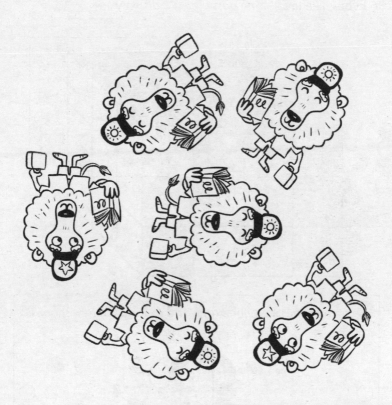

Can you work out how many building-block cubes there are in each of these 3D pictures? Make sure you don't forget to count any cubes that are hidden behind or underneath the cubes you can see.

Remember, each shape started off as a 4x3x3 arrangement of 36 cubes, like this:

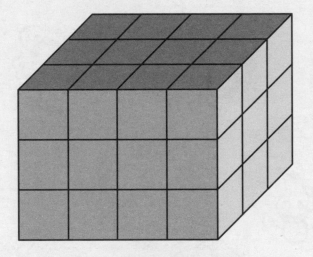

Some of the cubes were then removed to form the new shapes.

How many cubes are there in these pictures?

a)

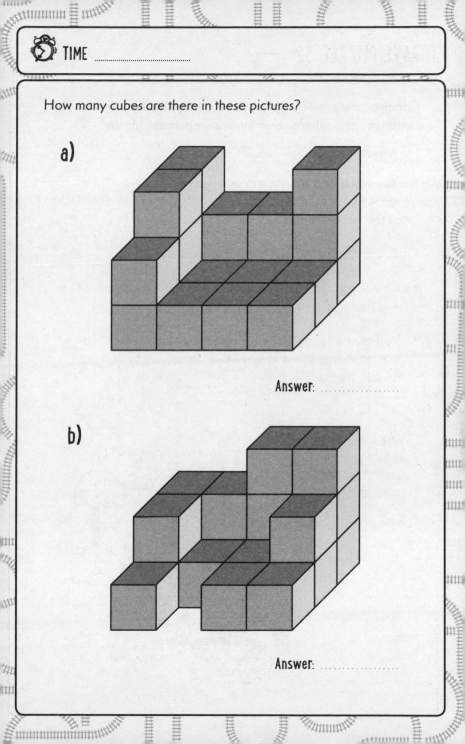

Answer: ....

b)

Answer: ....

Complete the puzzles on the opposite page by drawing lines to represent bridges between the numbered desert islands.

THE RULES

- You can only draw horizontal or vertical bridges, and each island must have the same number of bridges connected to it as the number printed inside the island.

- Bridges can't cross either each other or an island.

- One line represents one bridge. There can be no more than one bridge directly joining any pair of islands.

- You must arrange the set of bridges so that an animal could walk from one island to any other island, just by using the bridges that you've drawn.

Here's an example to help you understand how it works:

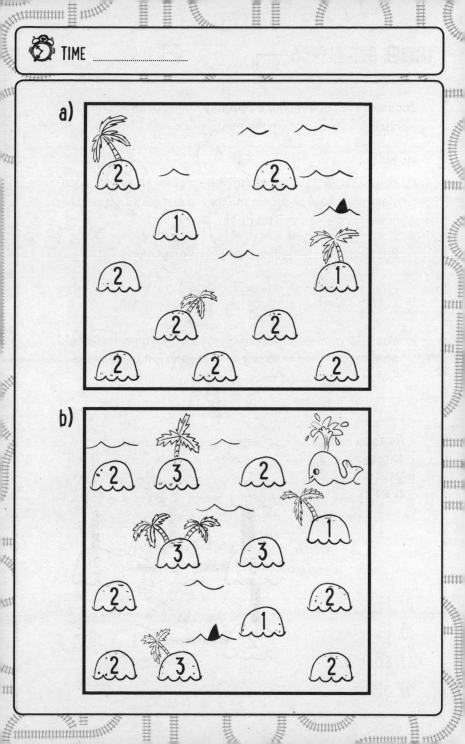

Each of these balloons has a different number painted on it.

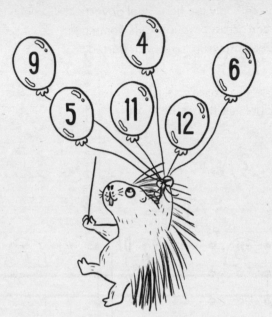

Can you work out which balloons you would have to pop so the numbers on the remaining balloons add together to form the totals below? For example, you could form a total of 9 by popping every balloon except 4 and 5, since 4 + 5 = 9. You can leave more than two balloons to reach your answer.

Which balloons would you leave to reach the following totals?

a) 14 ....

b) 19 ....

c) 28 ....

d) 35 ....

Can you draw straight lines to join all of the dots into a single loop? You can only use horizontal or vertical straight lines, and the loop can't cross or touch itself. Some parts of the loop have already been drawn in to get you started.

Here's an example solution.
Notice how it uses every dot:

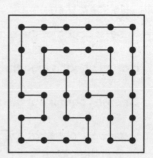

a)

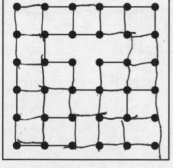

b)

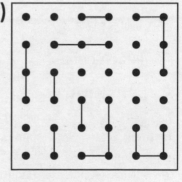

George, Harriet and Isabel are having a sailing race. Their boats are three different sizes. One is in the lead, one is in second place and one is in third place.

You also know that:

- Isabel is ahead of the biggest boat.

- Harriet's boat is bigger than the boat in third place.

- George's boat is not the smallest.

Can you work out what size of boat each sailor has and what their position in the race is?

George's boat is .... and is in .... place.

Harriet's boat is .... and is in .... place.

Isabel's boat is .... and is in .... place.

Reveal a hidden tropical creature by carefully colouring each shape in the picture below using this key:

1: Red   2: Yellow   3: Green   4: Brown

5: Black   6: Light blue   7: White   8: Orange

TIME ....

The owner of this camping site wants to attach one tent to each of his trees so that every tent sits in one of the grid squares immediately above, below, to the left or to the right of a tree. Can you help him work out where to put the tents?

THE RULES

- He doesn't want any tents to be in grid squares that are touching — and that includes diagonally touching squares, too.

- You can work out the solution by using his notes along the bottom and side of each grid, which show how many tents he must put in each row and column of the grid.

Here's an example solution to show you how it works:

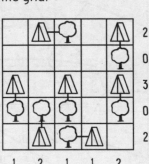

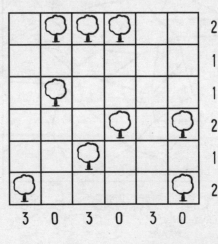

Can you build a word pyramid by solving the clues below? When solved, each row of the pyramid should contain the same set of letters as the row above plus one extra letter. The letters can be rearranged into a different order.

So, for example, you might have the word DOG on the top row. You can add an 'L' and rearrange the letters to make GOLD on the second row. Then you might add an 'E' and rearrange the letters to make the word LODGE on the third row, and so on, until the pyramid is filled.

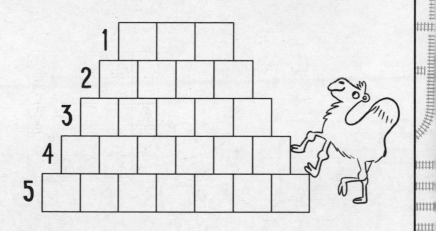

Here are clues for each row:

1) The highest point. You might say you have reached the '___' of the mountain or you are '___' of the class.

2) Don't go any further. Come to a '____'.

3) Football and baseball are both examples of this.

4) Something you might put on your bedroom wall.

5) Having the least amount of money.

This careful traveller has made sure he's well-protected from the sunshine by buying several hats and pairs of sunglasses. All the hats were one price and all the sunglasses were another price. By looking at these bills, can you work out how much each hat and each pair of sunglasses cost?

4 hats + 1 pair of sunglasses = £28

2 hats + 2 pairs of sunglasses = £26

1 hat = ...

1 pair of sunglasses = ...

Can you find all of these airport-related words in the grid below? They may be written in any direction: forwards, backwards, up, down or diagonally.

```
T E Y F P A S S P O R T S A A
S T N A R U A T S E R A N R O
R I S C L O U N G E A N U K I
X S N I K C E H C E O S C N X
R L U S N N U T R U S E O E D
C A Y R K E I A N E N I S E I
T V C T D C G C C I T M P C I
A I R I K N E U H A O A E E S
U R S E I M R C R T R G S E I
I R T T E I A G S T A R R A
E A I N T M I U U G T K S F E
R A T Y Y M C R G I U S E Y A
W S C A M M E U E P A N S T S
R L R I A S L N A Y T P H U T
R X M N O I T C E P S N I D C
```

ANNOUNCEMENTS	IMMIGRATION	SECURITY
ARRIVALS	INSPECTION	TICKET
CHECK-IN	LOUNGE	WAITING AREA
CUSTOMS	LUGGAGE	X-RAY MACHINE
DEPARTURES	PASSPORTS	
DUTY FREE	RESTAURANTS	

TIME ....

Place a number from 1 to 6 into each empty square, so that each number appears once in every row and column. Identical numbers can't touch – not even diagonally.

a)

	4	6	2	1	
2					6
3		4	1		5
4		5	3		1
6					2
	5	2	6	3	

b)

		2	3		
	3			6	
	1			2	
		3	5		

Help the seagull count the number of planes in this image.

Each plane looks like this:

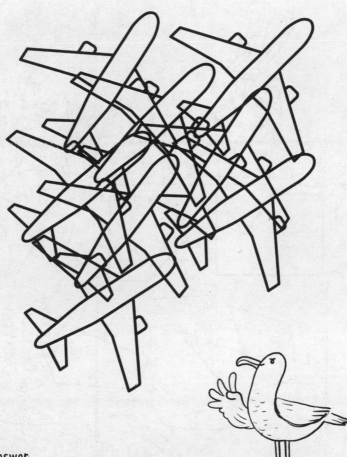

Answer: ....

Look carefully at the shape of each of these five stepping stones. Can you work out which one is the odd one out, and why?

Answer: ....

Help the lemur through the maze to get to the ice-cream van.

Start

Finish

Can you solve this sneaky silhouette challenge and work out which of the images below exactly matches the fox? The silhouettes may all look the same but only one is a perfect match.

a)

b)

c)

d)

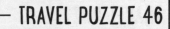

Can you fit all of these island-themed words into this grid, placing each word either horizontally or vertically?

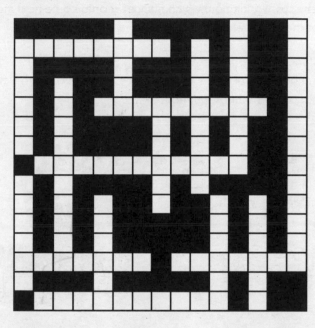

5-letter word
FAROE

6-letter words
AEGEAN
CANARY
FIJIAN
IONIAN
SAMOAN
TUVALU

7-letter words
AEOLIAN
LEEWARD

8-letter words
BALEARIC
FALKLAND
HAWAIIAN

9-letter word
MELANESIA

10-letter words
PHILIPPINE
POLYNESIAN

11-letter word
MICRONESIAN

13-letter word
BRITISH VIRGIN

TRAVEL PUZZLE 47 →

These animals have been having so much fun on holiday, they've forgotten how many days they've been away. Can you help them remember by working out which number should come next in each of these sequences?

For instance, in the first sequence – 15, 17, 19, 21, 23, 25 – the next number is 27 because the sequence is 'add 2 at each step'. But what are the other sequences?

a)

Solve these sudoku puzzles by placing a number from 1 to 6 in each empty square. Once complete, every row, column and bold-lined 3x2 box must contain each number from 1 to 6.

a)

2		6	1		3
3					1
6					5
1		3	6		4

b)

1		5	2		4
	4			5	
3					2
5					3
	2			3	
4		3	1		6

Can you draw along the grid lines to divide these rectangles up into five separate areas? Each area should contain one A, one B, one C and one D.

Here's an example.
Notice how each area has
four different letters in it:

D	A	B	D	C
B	D	C	C	A
D	B	A	B	B
C	A	C	D	A

a)

C	D	D	D	B
D	A	B	A	C
C	B	A	C	B
B	A	D	A	C

b)

A	B	B	D	A
A	C	D	A	C
D	B	C	B	C
A	B	C	D	D

TIME ....

Join the dots to reveal a piece of footwear you might spot on a beach. Start at 1 and draw a straight line to 2, then to 3 and so on, until you reach dot 48. What have you drawn?

Using your knowledge of the world, can you write a number next to each country to show what continent it is in? There are more countries than continents listed, so some continents will be used more than once — and some may not be used at all!

Continents

OCEANIA	ANTARCTICA	ASIA	AFRICA
1	2	3	4

EUROPE	NORTH AMERICA	SOUTH AMERICA
5	6	7

Countries

Algeria ...	France ...	Morocco ...
Argentina ...	Germany ...	New Zealand ...
Australia ...	India ...	South Korea ...
Brazil ...	Italy ...	Switzerland ...
Canada ...	Japan ...	United Kingdom ...
China ...	Mexico ...	United States ...

The letters in each of the words below have been scrambled up. Can you rearrange each set of letters to spell the name of a vehicle? For example, BSU could be rearranged to spell BUS.

a) ACR

b) ABOT

c) AITX

d) AELNP

e) CEEHILOPRT

TRAVEL PUZZLE 53

These pictures look identical at first glance, but there are in fact 12 differences between them. Can you find them all?

TRAVEL PUZZLE 54 →

Complete the puzzles on the opposite page by drawing lines to represent bridges between the numbered desert islands.

THE RULES

- You can only draw horizontal or vertical bridges, and each island must have the same number of bridges connected to it as the number printed inside the island.

- Bridges can't cross either each other or an island.

- One line represents one bridge. There can be no more than one bridge directly joining any pair of islands.

- You must arrange the set of bridges so that an animal could walk from one island to any other island, just by using the bridges that you've drawn.

Here's an example to help you understand how it works:

Can you solve the number pyramids on these sun loungers? Each square should contain a number that is equal to the sum of the two blocks immediately beneath it.

a)

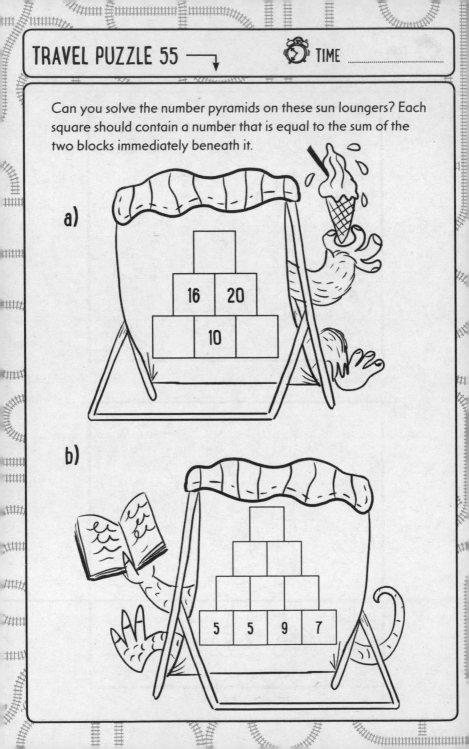

16	20

| 10 |

b)

| 5 | 5 | 9 | 7 |

Daniel, Emma and Francis have all got on a train at the same stop. One of them will get off at the second stop, one will get off at the fourth stop and one will get off at the eighth stop.

You know that one of them is going to the beach, one is going to a museum and one is going to the zoo.

You have also been given these facts:

- The traveller who's going to the beach will get off sooner than Emma.

- Daniel will be on the train for twice as many stops as Francis.

- The traveller who's going to the beach will be on the train for longer than the traveller who's going to the museum.

Based on this information, can you work out at which stop each traveller is getting off and where they are going?

Daniel is getting off at .... and is going to ....

Emma is getting off at .... and is going to ....

Francis is getting off at .... and is going to ....

Can you join all of these circles into pairs? Each pair should contain one white circle and one shaded circle.

THE RULES

- Lines cannot cross over each other or cross over other circles.
- Only horizontal and vertical lines are allowed.
- Every circle must form part of one pair only.

Here's an example to show you how it works:

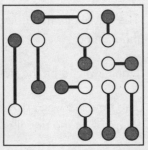

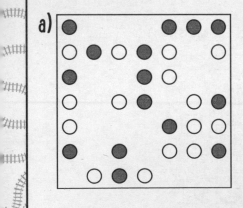

a)

b)

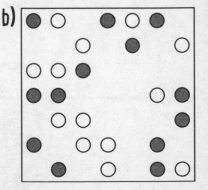

Help the family of moose through the maze to find their hotel.

Start

Finish

TRAVEL PUZZLE 59 →

Can you find all of these language-themed words in the grid below? They may be written in any direction: forwards, backwards, up, down or diagonally.

E	S	D	B	A	T	U	T	A	P	E	N	N	R	P
N	N	A	I	L	A	T	I	N	A	H	H	I	I	A
G	N	U	C	M	E	R	T	H	N	A	H	S	A	P
L	S	R	H	A	I	P	S	T	R	S	T	H	R	H
I	N	U	L	N	K	B	P	K	I	H	G	L	E	M
S	K	S	G	D	I	G	R	K	N	I	S	S	E	P
H	N	S	E	A	A	N	R	S	H	A	E	S	U	I
S	A	I	R	R	T	U	S	S	R	N	E	N	T	H
K	E	A	M	I	T	I	I	A	A	N	J	H	S	N
N	R	N	A	N	A	N	R	P	O	A	C	I	N	E
H	O	I	N	H	A	L	A	T	B	N	L	N	H	L
S	K	R	T	P	H	J	N	I	E	O	P	R	I	I
T	I	I	S	K	U	A	N	R	P	N	A	A	N	H
S	N	A	J	A	C	S	F	C	I	B	A	R	A	N
I	D	N	I	H	I	A	J	N	A	I	T	C	S	G

ARABIC	ITALIAN	PUNJABI
CANTONESE	JAPANESE	RUSSIAN
ENGLISH	KOREAN	SPANISH
FRENCH	MANDARIN	THAI
GERMAN	POLISH	TURKISH
HINDI		

Solve these odd-even sudoku puzzles by placing a number from 1 to 6 in each empty square. Every row, column and bold-lined 3x2 box must contain each number from 1 to 6. Shaded squares must contain even numbers (2, 4, 6) and unshaded squares must contain odd numbers (1, 3, 5).

a)

2					5
3					6
	2			1	

b)

5					6
	2			3	
	6			1	
3					2

Reveal a place you might visit on holiday by colouring in every triangle in the picture below. Leave the other shapes blank.

Can you crack the cunning code below? Shift each letter back by two letters in the alphabet to reveal an amazing fact about the Earth. Here's the alphabet to help you:

A B C D E F G H I J K L M N O P Q R S T U V W X Y Z

For example, you should change C to A, change D to B and so on. Wrap around the end of the alphabet, so that you also change A to Y and B to Z and so on. But don't change any of the punctuation or numbers.

Vjg nqyguv rqkpv qp Gctvj vjcv'u uvknn fta ncpf

ku vjg ujqtg qh vjg Fgcf Ugc, yjkej ku cdqwv

420 o (1,375 hv) dgnqy ugc ngxgn.

Can you solve these three brain chains in your head, without writing anything down? Start with the number at the top of each smoothie glass. Do what the maths instructions say in turn until you reach the empty space at the bottom. Write your answer in there.

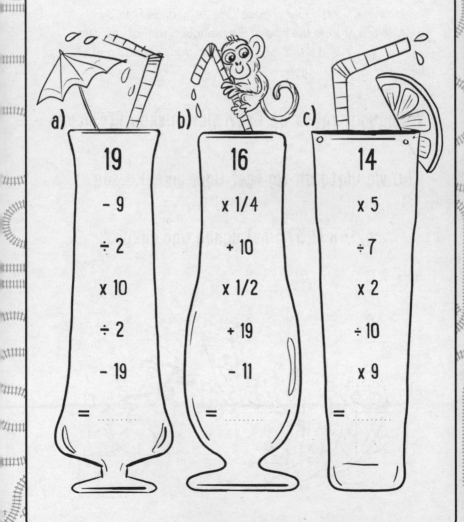

a)

19

− 9

÷ 2

x 10

÷ 2

− 19

= ....

b)

16

x 1/4

+ 10

x 1/2

+ 19

− 11

= ....

c)

14

x 5

÷ 7

x 2

÷ 10

x 9

= ....

If you folded up the image at the top of the page to make a cube, which of the four images at the bottom of the page would match that cube? A good way to tackle this puzzle is to first work out which cubes are clearly wrong. The remaining cube must be the correct one.

If you get stuck, you could draw a copy of the image, cut it out and fold it up.

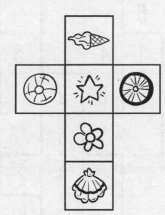

a)

b)

c)

d)

Can you solve these jigsaw sudoku puzzles by placing a number from 1 to 6 in each empty square. Every row, column and bold-lined jigsaw shape must contain each number from 1 to 6.

a)

1	6				5
2	1	4		3	
4		6	2		
		1	6		4
	3		4	2	1
5				6	2

b)

1		3			2
	1			3	
6		5	4		
		2	1		6
	3			5	
4			3		5

Can you build a word pyramid by solving each of the clues? When solved, each row of the pyramid should contain the same set of letters as the row above plus one extra letter. The letters can be rearranged into a different order.

For example, you might have CAT on the top row, then add an 'R' and rearrange the letters to make CART. Next, you might add an 'E' and rearrange again to make CRATE, and so on, until the pyramid is filled.

Here are clues for each row:

1) A small, crawling insect that lives in a large colony.

2) Very tidy and well-arranged.

3) A spy is also known as a 'secret _____'.

4) A special piece of metal that sticks to other pieces of metal.

5) A shade of pinkish purple.

In the puzzles below, can you draw a single loop that passes through the centre of every white square, using only horizontal and vertical lines? The loop cannot cross over either itself or pass through a black square, or visit any square more than once.

Here's an example solution. Notice how the line passes through the centre of every white square:

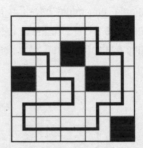

a)

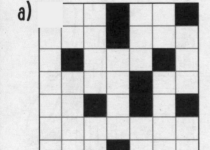

b)

Oh dear — this rabbit has forgotten which hotel room she's staying in. You need to work out which lock will be opened by this key. By looking at the profiles of the locks below, can you work out which one the key will slot into perfectly?

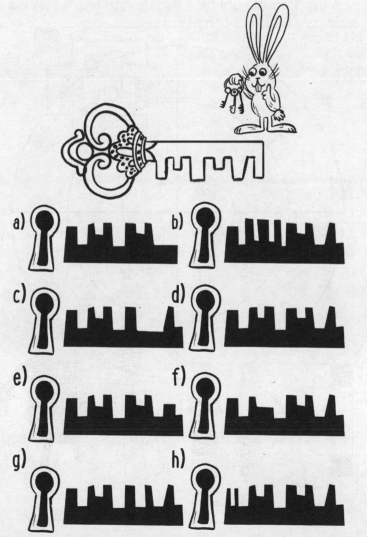

TIME ....

Can you form the target sums below by choosing one number from each ring of the dartboard and then adding them together?

For example, you could form a sum of 14 by picking 2 from the inner ring, 5 from the middle ring and 7 from the outer ring. You can reuse numbers to make different target sums.

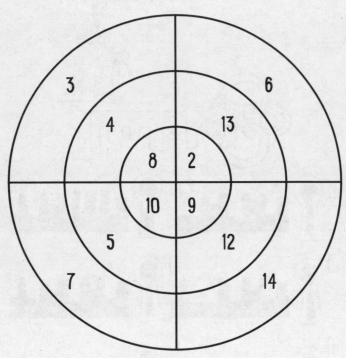

TARGET SUMS:

15 = ...

23 = ...

30 = ...

Solve these futoshiki puzzles by placing the numbers 1 to 5 once each into every row and column. But be sure to obey the 'greater than' signs. These are arrows that always point from the bigger number to the smaller number of a pair. For example, you could have '3 > 1' since 3 is greater than 1, but '1 > 2' would be wrong because 1 is not greater in value than 2.

a)

b)

How many words can you find in this word square?

Start on any letter, then move in any direction (including diagonally) to a touching letter. Keep moving to touching letters until you have spelled out a word of three or more letters, but without visiting any square more than once within the word. Can you find the one word that uses all of the letters?

GOOD: 15 words
EXCELLENT: 25 words
FANTASTIC: 35 words

B	R	T
N	A	S
I	I	E

Can you help this peacock find his way through the giant maze to reach his family?

Start

Finish

This holiday maker is at a market picking up some fruit.
Using these sums, can you work out how much each type
of fruit sells for?

2 apples + 3 oranges = 17 cents

1 pineapple + 2 oranges = 14 cents

4 apples + 2 pineapples = 32 cents

1 apple costs = ...

1 orange costs = ...

1 pineapple costs = ...

The owner of this camping site wants to attach one tent to each of his trees so that each tent sits in one of the grid squares immediately above, below, to the left or to the right of a tree. Can you help him work out where to put them?

THE RULES

- To ensure privacy, he doesn't want any tents to be in grid squares that are touching – and that includes diagonally touching squares, too.

- You can work out the solution by using his notes around the side of the grid, which show how many tents he must put in each row and column.

Here's an example solution to show you how it can be done:

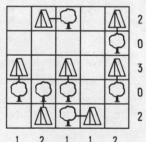

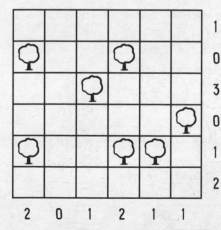

Three families – the Briscoe family, the Dyson family and the Walker family – are all driving along the motorway. One family has one child in their car, another family has two children in their car and the remaining family has three children in their car.

The families are all alongside one another in three lanes of the motorway. The lanes are numbered, and one family is in lane 1, another family is in lane 2 and the remaining family is in lane 3.

You also know the following:

- No family is in a lane which matches the number of children they have in their car.

- The Dyson family have more children in their car than the family in lane 1.

- The Walker family are in a lower-numbered lane than the family with one child in their car.

- The Dyson family have an odd number of children in their car.

Can you work out which lane each family is in, and how many children they have in their car?

The Briscoe family are in lane .... and have ....

The Dyson family are in lane .... and have ....

The Walker family are in lane .... and have ....

Can you fit all of the countries listed below into this grid, placing each word either horizontally or vertically?

4-letter words	LIBYA	ECUADOR
CHAD	MALTA	ESTONIA
FIJI	YEMEN	FINLAND
IRAN		
IRAQ	6-letter words	9-letter words
	CANADA	INDONESIA
5-letter words	ISRAEL	LITHUANIA
BENIN	JORDAN	SINGAPORE
CHINA	TURKEY	
EGYPT		10-letter word
INDIA	7-letter words	BANGLADESH
KENYA	CROATIA	
	DENMARK	

Solve these kakuro puzzles by writing a number from 1 to 9 into each of the white squares.

THE RULES

- Place the numbers so that each continuous horizontal or vertical run of white squares adds up to the clue number shown in the shaded square to the left or top of that run.

- If a clue number appears above the diagonal line then it gives the total of the run to its right. If it appears below the diagonal line, then it gives the total of the run directly below the clue.

- You can't repeat a number in any continuous run of white squares. For example, to solve the clue number '4', you would have to use '3' and '1' as '2' and '2' would mean repeating '2'.

a)

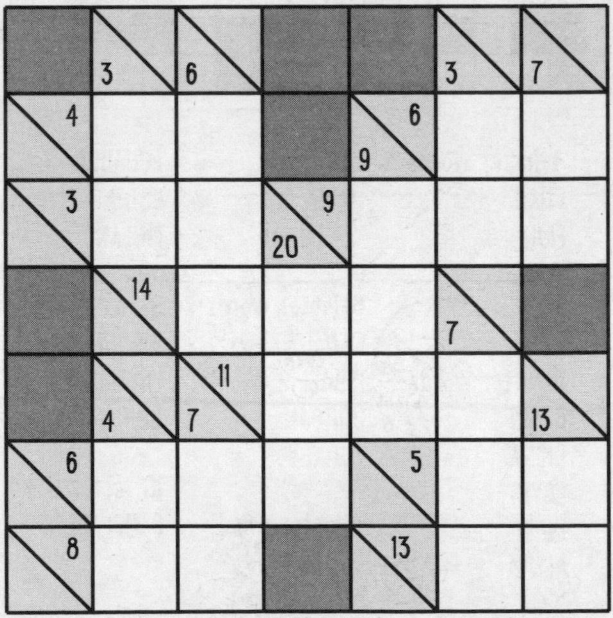

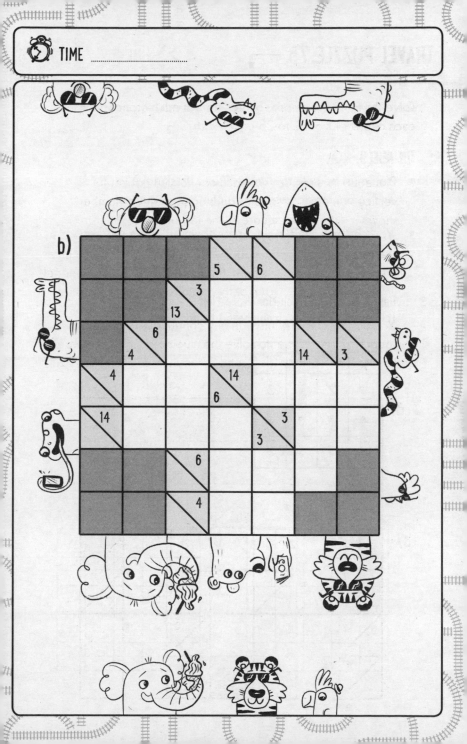

b)

Can you fill in the empty squares so that each grid contains every number from 1 to 25 once each?

THE RULES

- You must be able to start at '1' and then move to '2', '3', '4' and so on, moving only to touching grid squares.

- You can move left, right, up or down between squares, but not diagonally.

Here's an example solution. Note that this example just uses numbers 1 to 16:

10	9	8	1
11	12	7	2
16	13	6	3
15	14	5	4

a)

	2		20	
4	1		21	24
		17		
8	7		15	14
	10		12	

b)

21					3
			6		
	18	17	8		
		16			
25				11	

This mole is trying to find his way back to his beach towel after a swim. The trouble is, he can't remember which one it was. They all look identical. Can you find the towel that's slightly different to the others?

Place a number from 1 to 6 into each empty square, so that each number appears once in every row and column. Identical numbers can't touch — not even diagonally.

a)

	3			1	
4					6
		4	1		
		2	3		
6					3
	2			4	

b)

2		4	6		5
4					1
5					3
6		5	2		4

This area on the beach has three different types of ball in it – basketballs, footballs and tennis balls.

Can you draw three straight lines to divide the beach into four areas, so that each area contains exactly one of each type of ball? The lines must go from one side of the area to the other.

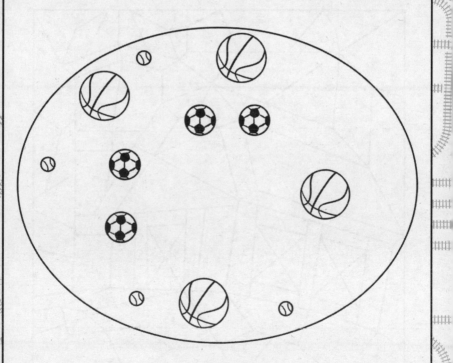

Can you reveal a hidden rural scene by colouring each shape in the picture using this key:

1: Light blue   2: Light green   3: Dark green   4: Yellow

5: Orange   6: Light grey   7: Red   8: Black

Can you find the names of all these currencies in the grid below?
They may be written in any direction: forwards, backwards, up,
down or diagonally.

```
P E R N E K D U L R R T O N U
L O N N O P E R D E E R A E L
L K R F O N I A O N K E L E K
O A D W L E R L P N R E P A F
L I E K K Y O L I E N L H U A
A R O R L A D O L R L D F S R
O E R C R O Z D U R Z T R D R
R N R O K N P O U N D N Z N N
P N S O E O D A R E E I R A N
W E U P O W R N U L E R O R E
P E P A E N E T H D A O Z O C
I E O U O N U Y W O I F R C O
T Y T O L Z O E U R O N N O F
O I R L U R O R Y L F R A N C
F A R N D L L F K N O O R R R
```

DINAR	FRANC	POUND	SHEKEL
DOLLAR	KRONE	RAND	WON
EURO	LEU	REAL	YEN
FORINT	PESO	RUPEE	ZLOTY

Can you draw along the grid lines to divide these rectangles up into seven separate areas? Each area should contain one A, one B, one C and one D.

Here's an example solution, which only has five areas. Notice how each area has four different letters in it:

D	A	B	D	C
B	D	C	C	A
D	B	A	B	B
C	A	C	D	A

a)

B	C	D	C	B	A	D
B	D	A	B	B	D	A
A	C	C	D	D	C	C
D	B	A	A	A	C	B

b)

C	A	B	B	D	D	A
C	C	D	D	C	C	C
D	A	D	A	A	A	D
A	B	B	B	C	B	B

Using your knowledge of the world, can you draw a line to join each country to the name of its currency? One of the lines has been drawn in already to show you how it works.

You might find this puzzle tricky, so don't worry if you need to ask for help!

COUNTRY	CURRENCY
Australia	Dollar
Brazil	Euro
China	Forint
Denmark	Franc
Egypt	Krone
France	Peso
Hungary	Pound
India	Rand
Mexico	Real
Russia	Rouble
South Africa	Rupee
South Korea	Won
Switzerland	Yuan

Can you draw paths to connect each pair of identical objects together on the grids on the opposite page? The paths must be made up of horizontal and vertical lines, and can't cross or touch each other. No more than one path can enter any grid square.

This finished puzzle
shows you how it works:

Each pair of objects
is linked together ⟶
by a path made
of horizontal and
vertical lines.

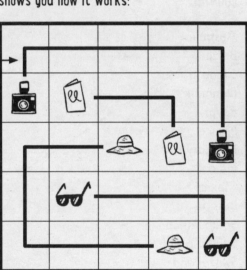

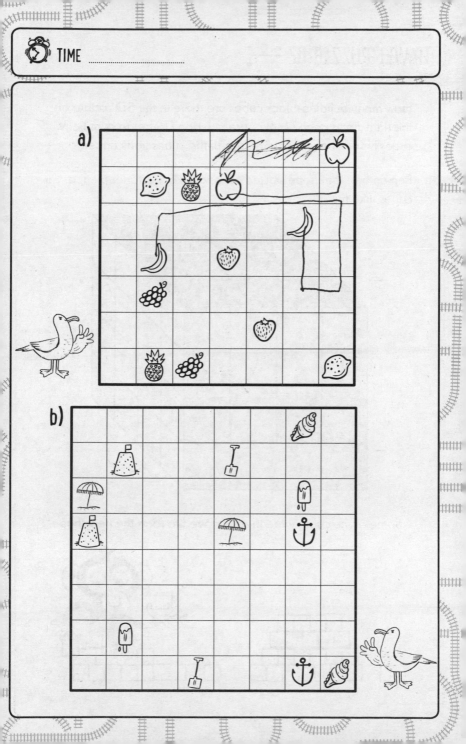

How many building-block cubes are there in the 3D picture on the right-hand page? Make sure you don't forget to count any cubes hidden behind or underneath the cubes you can see.

Remember, the shape started off as a 4x4x4 arrangement of 64 cubes, like this:

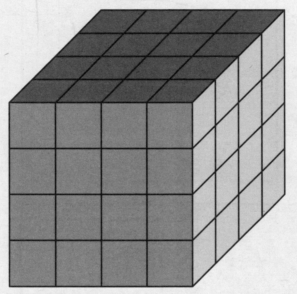

Some of the cubes were then removed to form the new shape.

How many cubes are there in this picture?

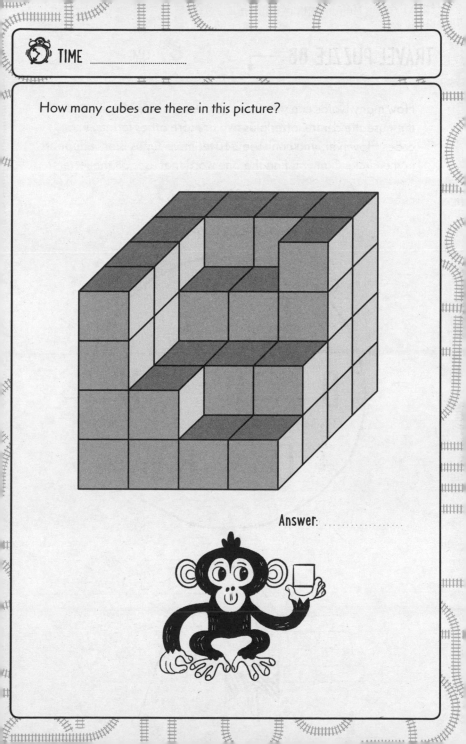

Answer:

How many words can you find in this word circle? Each word must use the centre letter plus two or more other letters, in any order. However, you can't use a letter more times than it appears in the circle. Can you find the one word that uses all the letters?

EASY TARGET: 8 words
EXCELLENT TARGET: 13 words
SUPERB TARGET: 18 words

Each of these balloons has a different number painted on it.

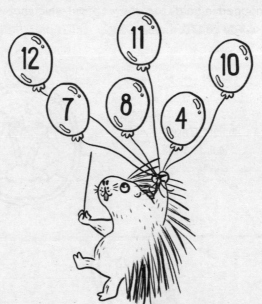

Can you work out which balloons you would have to pop so the numbers on the remaining balloons add together to form the totals below? For example, you could form a total of 12 by popping every balloon except 4 and 8, because 4 + 8 = 12. You can leave more than two balloons to reach your answer.

Which balloons would you leave to reach the following totals?

a) 17 ....

b) 20 ....

c) 32 ....

d) 38 ....

Oops – the trinkets you bought on holiday to bring back as gifts have all snapped in half! Can you work out which halves go together, so you can fix them?

A complete trinket should look like this:

Can you solve these jigsaw sudoku puzzles by placing a number from 1 to 6 in each empty square. Once complete, every row, column and bold-lined jigsaw shape must contain each number from 1 to 6.

a)

6	5		3		2
2		5		6	
	2		1		
		2		1	
	6		2		1
1		3		2	6

b)

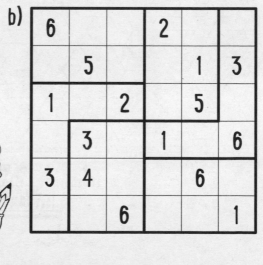

6			2		
	5			1	3
1		2		5	
	3		1		6
3	4			6	
		6			1

Help the mice find the way to their cruise ship by tracing a path through this triangular maze.

Start

Finish

Abby, Ben and Conchita are on the train together. From the following conversation, can you work out how old each of them is?

- Conchita says, 'I'm younger than 16.'

- Abby says, 'I'm seven years younger than you, Conchita.'

- Ben says, 'And I'm exactly one and a half times Abby's age.'

- Abby says, 'Conchita is less than twice as old as I am.'

Abby is .... years old.

Ben is .... years old.

Conchita is .... years old.

Can you draw straight lines to join all of the dots into a single loop? You can only use horizontal or vertical straight lines, and the loop can't cross or touch itself. Some parts of the loop have already been drawn in to get you started.

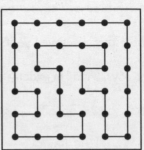

Here's an example solution.
Notice how it uses every dot:

a)

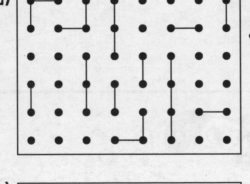

b)

Look carefully at the shape of each of these five stepping stones.
Can you work out which one is the odd one out, and why?

Answer: ....

Can you build a word pyramid by solving each of the clues? When solved, each row should contain the same set of letters as the row above plus one extra letter. The letters can be rearranged into a different order.

So, for example, you might have the word DOG on the top row. You can add an 'L' and rearrange the letters to make GOLD on the second row. Then you might add an 'E' and rearrange the letters to make the word LODGE on the third row, and so on, until the pyramid is filled.

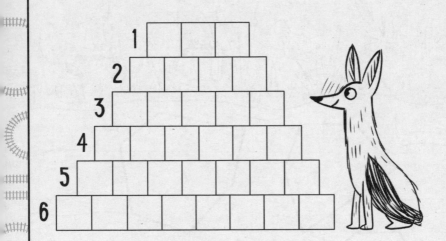

Here are clues for each row:

1) Observe with your eyes.

2) You can grow a plant from this.

3) Tall grasses that grow by rivers.

4) Deleted; rubbed out.

5) Oiled something.

6) To have a different opinion.

Different countries of the world often use different time zones, meaning that when it's one time in one country it can be a different time in another. Really big countries often have multiple time zones. So, for example, the United States has 6 different time zones and Russia has 11 different time zones!

The time on the East Coast of the US is 5 hours behind the time in the United Kingdom. This means that when it is 11am in the United Kingdom, it's 6am in the United States. Bearing that in mind, can you solve the following problems?

1) When it's 3pm on the East Coast of the US what time is it in the UK?

Answer: ....

2) When it's midnight in the UK, what time is it on the East Coast of the US?

Answer: ....

Solve these kakuro puzzles by writing a number from 1 to 9 into each of the white squares.

THE RULES

- Place the numbers so that each continuous horizontal or vertical run of white squares adds up to the clue number shown in the shaded square to the left or top of that run.

- If a clue number appears above the diagonal line then it gives the total of the run to its right. If it appears below the diagonal line, then it gives the total of the run directly below the clue.

- You can't repeat a number in any continuous run of white squares. For example, to solve the clue number '4', you would have to use '3' and '1' as '2' and '2' would mean repeating '2'.

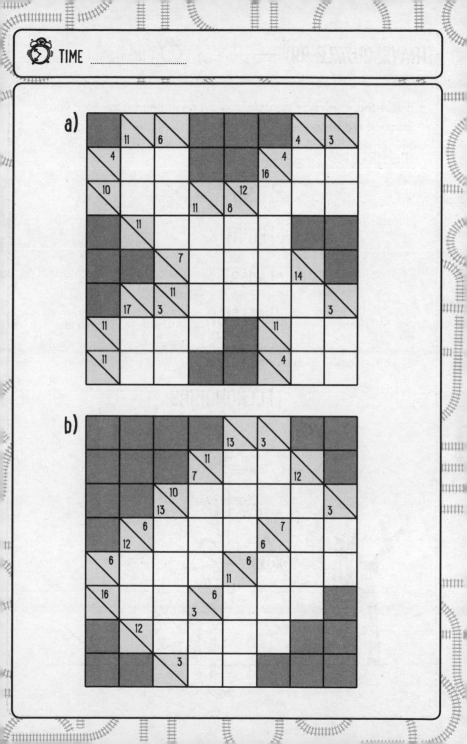

The letters in each of the words below have been scrambled up. Can you rearrange each set of letters to spell the name of an animal you might see on safari? For example, CHIORST could be rearranged to spell OSTRICH.

a) ILNO

b) EGIRT

c) ABERZ

d) AEFFIGR

e) AEEHLNPT

f) CEHONOIRRS

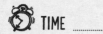

There are three flights leaving from an airport. One is going to London, one is going to Paris and one is going to Rome.

These flights are leaving from three different gates: gate 20, gate 26 and gate 31. You also know that the departure times for these three flights are 10:15, 10:40 and 11:00.

You have also been given these facts:

- The flight to London is leaving after the flight to Paris.

- The 10:40 flight has a higher gate number than the flight to Rome.

- The flight from gate 20 is not leaving at 10:15.

- The flight to Rome has a higher gate number than the 11:00 flight.

Based on these details, can you work out from which gate each of the three flights is leaving and the departure time of each flight?

The flight to London is leaving from gate ...... at ....

The flight to Paris is leaving from gate ...... at ....

The flight to Rome is leaving from gate ...... at ....

Colour in every triangle in the picture below, while leaving the other shapes blank. What magical image do you reveal?

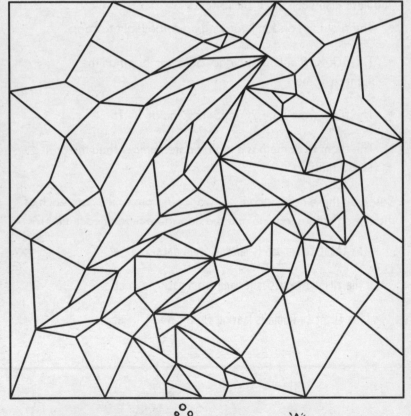

All
of the
ANSWERS

TRAVEL PUZZLE 1

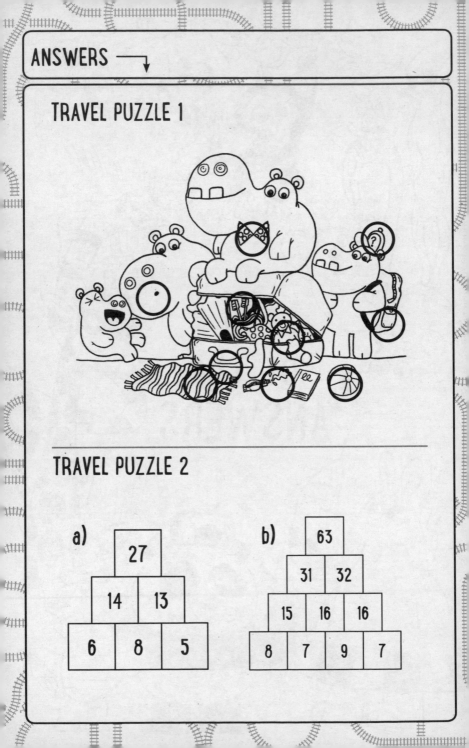

TRAVEL PUZZLE 2

a)

	27	
14		13
6	8	5

b)

		63		
	31		32	
15		16		16
8	7		9	7

TRAVEL PUZZLE 3

Argentina – Buenos Aires
Australia – Canberra
Canada – Ottawa
China – Beijing
India – New Delhi
Kenya – Nairobi
Russia – Moscow

TRAVEL PUZZLE 4

a)

4	2	1	3
1	3	4	2
2	1	3	4
3	4	2	1

b)

4	3	1	2
2	1	4	3
3	4	2	1
1	2	3	4

c)

1	4	2	3
3	2	4	1
4	3	1	2
2	1	3	4

TRAVEL PUZZLE 5

The hottest place on Earth is Death Valley in the United States. An air temperature of 56.7°C (134°F) was once recorded there!

TRAVEL PUZZLE 6

Cube b is the correct one. On cube a the tree and mountain are swapped over. On cube c the tree could not be next to the owl. On cube d the boat and mountain are swapped over.

TRAVEL PUZZLE 7

The 9-letter word is triangles.

Other words to be found include air, angle, angler, angles, ant, anti (someone who is opposed to something), antler, ants, ate, eta (a Greek letter), gnat, gnats, inlet, inlets, ire (anger), its, lei (a Hawaiian garland), lest, let, lets, nit, nits, rein, rest, resting, retain, retina, ring, ringlet, ringlets, rite, rites, set, stain, stair, sting, stir, string, tan, tang (a strong taste), tangle, tangles, tie, tier, ties, tin, ting (a ringing sound), tingle, tingles, tire, tires, triangle and tries.

TRAVEL PUZZLE 8

A flamingo

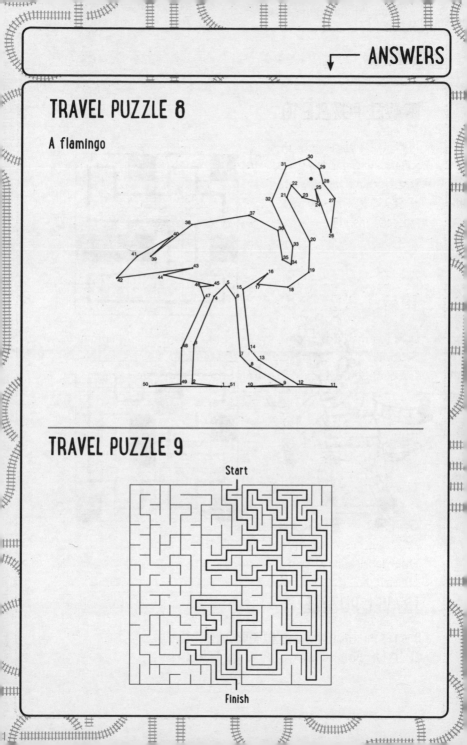

TRAVEL PUZZLE 9

Start

Finish

TRAVEL PUZZLE 10

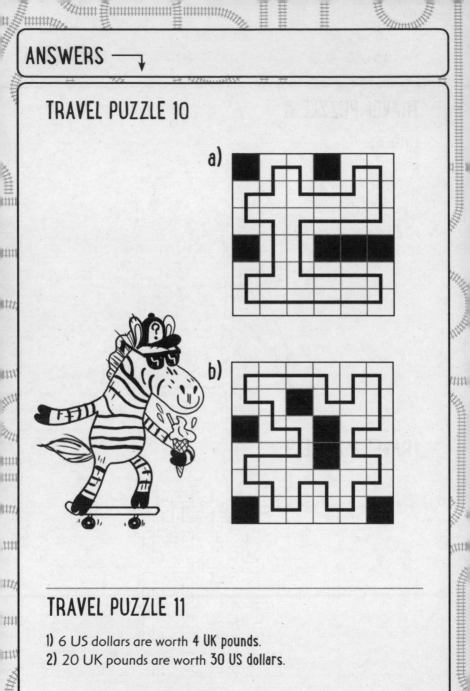

a)

b)

TRAVEL PUZZLE 11

1) 6 US dollars are worth **4 UK pounds.**
2) 20 UK pounds are worth **30 US dollars.**

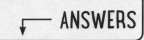

TRAVEL PUZZLE 12

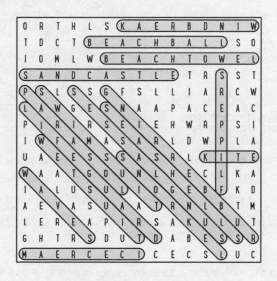

TRAVEL PUZZLE 13

a)

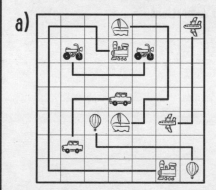

b)

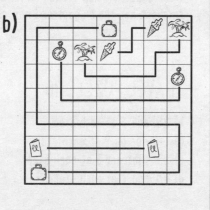

TRAVEL PUZZLE 14

There are **7 suitcases**:
3 larger ones and
4 smaller ones.

TRAVEL PUZZLE 15

Beth's castle is bigger than Catherine's, but Catherine's is not the smallest — so Alex must have the smallest castle, and therefore Beth has the biggest one. We also know that the smallest castle, Alex's, has shells on it. Catherine's castle doesn't have stones on it, so it must be Beth's castle that has the stones.

You could also solve this puzzle by experimenting with different options, and seeing if they fit the clues. There aren't too many possible combinations. The correct answer is:

Alex's castle is the smallest and has shells on it. Beth's castle is the biggest and has stones on it. Catherine's castle is neither the smallest nor the biggest and has no decorations.

TRAVEL PUZZLE 16

a) 20: add 3 at each step
b) 1: divide by 2 at each step
c) 33: subtract 3 at each step
d) 48: add 7 at each step

ANSWERS

TRAVEL PUZZLE 17

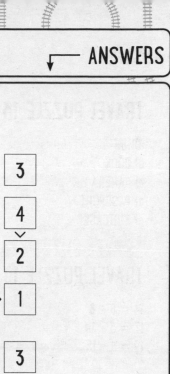

a)

1	4	2	3
2	1	3	4
4 > 3	1	2
3	2	4 > 1

b)

4	1 < 2	3
3	2	1	4
1	3	4	2
2 < 4	3 > 1

c)

4	3	2	1
1	2	3 < 4
2	1	4	3
3 < 4	1 < 2

TRAVEL PUZZLE 18

a) HAT
b) BOOK
c) CAMERA
d) PASSPORT
e) SUITCASE

TRAVEL PUZZLE 19

$14 = 6 + 8$
$17 = 3 + 14$
$19 = 6 + 13$

TRAVEL PUZZLE 20

The completed jigsaw would look like this. The shaded piece is the one that's missing.

TRAVEL PUZZLE 21

a)

13	12	5	4
14	11	6	3
15	10	7	2
16	9	8	1

b)

16	13	12	11
15	14	1	10
4	3	2	9
5	6	7	8

TRAVEL PUZZLE 22

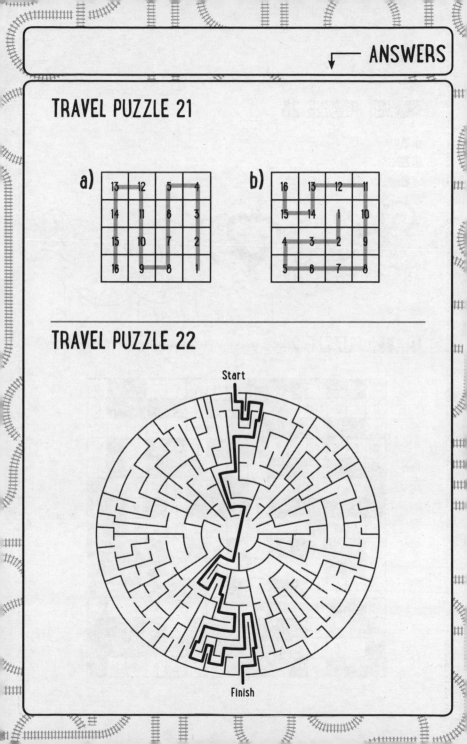

Start

Finish

TRAVEL PUZZLE 23

a) 13
b) 20
c) 48

TRAVEL PUZZLE 24

```
P . C . . . R I V E R . . G
O C E A N . . . E . . . . O
. V . . . . G L A C I E R R
D E S E R T . . D . . S . G
. R . . S E A . . . . L . E
. T U N D R A . . P E A K .
. . . . . V . . . L . . N .
B A Y . G R A S S L A N D .
E . . . N . . W . I . . . .
A . M O U N T A I N . . . .
C A V E . . A . M . . . . .
H . A R C H I P E L A G O .
. . D . . . . . . A . . . .
. W O O D . . . . K . . . .
. . W . . . . S T E P P E .
```

TRAVEL PUZZLE 25

TRAVEL PUZZLE 26

a)

5	2	1	4	3	6
4	3	6	2	5	1
1	5	4	3	6	2
3	6	2	5	1	4
2	1	3	6	4	5
6	4	5	1	2	3

b)

6	2	4	3	5	1
5	3	1	2	6	4
2	4	3	6	1	5
1	6	5	4	3	2
4	1	6	5	2	3
3	5	2	1	4	6

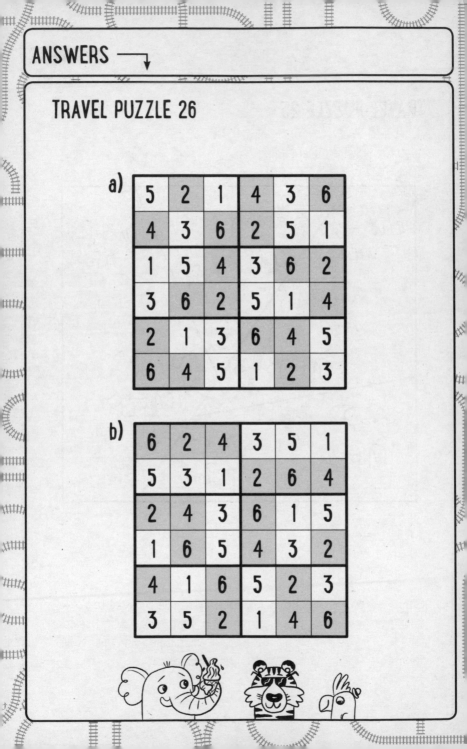

TRAVEL PUZZLE 27

Australia – Sydney Opera House
China – Great Wall
France – Eiffel Tower
Greece – Acropolis
India – Taj Mahal
Italy – Colosseum
Russia – Red Square
United Kingdom – Stonehenge
United States – Statue of Liberty

TRAVEL PUZZLE 28

The 7-letter word is **strains**.

Other words to be found include **ant, anti** (to be opposed to something), **ants, nit, nits, rain, rains, ran, rant, rants, saint, saints, sans** (a fancy way of saying 'without'), **satin, satins, sin, sins, stain, stains, strain, tan, tans, tin, tins, train** and **trains**.

TRAVEL PUZZLE 29

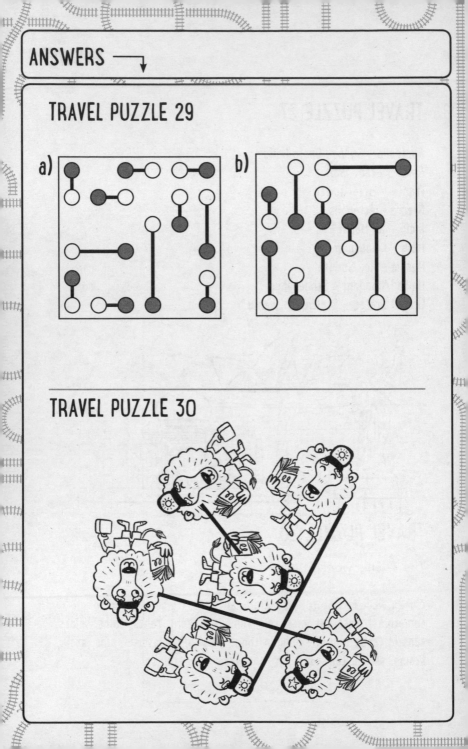

a)

b)

TRAVEL PUZZLE 30

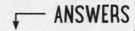
TRAVEL PUZZLE 31

a) There are 21 cubes: 3 cubes on the top layer, 6 cubes on the middle layer and 12 cubes on the bottom layer.

b) There 19 cubes: 2 cubes on the top layer, 6 cubes on the middle layer and 11 cubes on the bottom layer.

TRAVEL PUZZLE 32

a)

b)

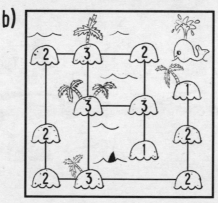

TRAVEL PUZZLE 33

$14 = 5 + 9$ (burst 4, 6, 11 and 12)
$19 = 4 + 6 + 9$ (burst 11, 5 and 12)
$28 = 5 + 11 + 12$ (burst 4, 9 and 6)
$35 = 4 + 5 + 6 + 9 + 11$ (burst 12)

TRAVEL PUZZLE 34

a)

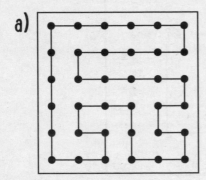

b)

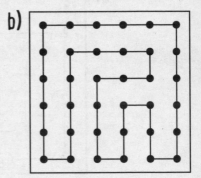

TRAVEL PUZZLE 35

Harriet's boat is bigger than another, and George's boat is not the smallest, so the smallest boat must be Isabel's. We know that Isabel is ahead of the biggest boat, and Harriet is not in third place, so the person in third place must be George. From this, we know that George, in third place, is not in the smallest boat. We also know that Harriet's boat is bigger than the boat in third place, so Harriet's boat must be the largest, George's the middle-sized one and Isabel's the smallest. Isabel is ahead of the biggest boat, so Isabel must be in first place and Harriet must be in second place.

George's boat is medium-sized and is in third place. Harriet's boat is the biggest and is in second place. Isabel's boat is the smallest and is in first place.

TRAVEL PUZZLE 36

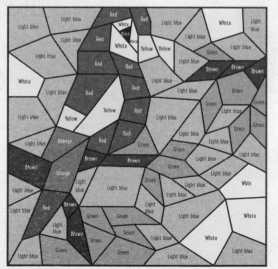

TRAVEL PUZZLE 37

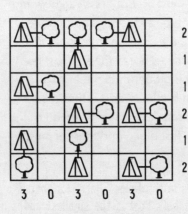

TRAVEL PUZZLE 38

1) TOP
2) STOP
3) SPORT
4) POSTER
5) POOREST

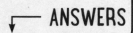

TRAVEL PUZZLE 39

One hat costs £5, and one pair of sunglasses costs £8.

TRAVEL PUZZLE 40

```
T E Y F P A S S P O R T S A A A
S T N A R U A T S E R A N R O
R I S C L O U N G E A N U K I
X S N I K C E H C E O S C N X
R L U S N N U T R U S E O E D
C A Y R K E I A N E N I S E I
T V C T D C G C C I T M P C I
A I R I K N E U H A O A E S I
U R S E I M R C R T R G S I A
I R T T E I A G S T A R R I A
E A I N T M I U U G T K S F E
R A T Y Y M C R G I U S E Y A
W S C A M M E U E P A N S T S
R L R I A S L N A Y T P H U T
R X M N O I T C E P S N I D C
```

TRAVEL PUZZLE 41

a)

5	4	6	2	1	3
2	1	3	5	4	6
3	6	4	1	2	5
4	2	5	3	6	1
6	3	1	4	5	2
1	5	2	6	3	4

b)

3	5	1	6	4	2
6	4	2	3	5	1
2	3	5	1	6	4
5	1	6	4	2	3
4	2	3	5	1	6
1	6	4	2	3	5

TRAVEL PUZZLE 42

There are **8** planes.

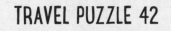

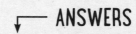
TRAVEL PUZZLE 43

Shape 2 is the odd one out because it has only five sides. All of the other shapes have six sides.

TRAVEL PUZZLE 44

Start

Finish

TRAVEL PUZZLE 45

Silhouette b

TRAVEL PUZZLE 46

```
. . . . . F . . . . . H . . . . B
F A L K L A N D . . B . H A W . . R
I . . P . R . . . . A . A . . . . I
J . . H M E L A N E S I A . . . . T
I . . I . E . A . . R . I . . . . I
A . . L . G . R . . I . A . . . . S
N . M I C R O N E S I A N . . . . H
. . . P . A . C . . . . . . . . . V
T . . P . . C . . . S . I . . . . I
U . . I . . A . . . A . O . . . . R
V . . N . . N . . . M . N . . . . G
A . . E . . R . . . . . . . . . . I
L . L E E W A R D . . A E O L I A N
U . . . . R . . . . . . . A . . . A
. . P O L Y N E S I A N . . . . . N
```

TRAVEL PUZZLE 47

a) 45: add 6 at each step
b) 27: subtract 12 at each step
c) 35: the difference between numbers increases by 1 at
   each step, so the sequence is + 3, + 4, + 5, + 6, + 7 and + 8
d) 76: add the previous two numbers at each step

TRAVEL PUZZLE 48

a)

2	5	6	1	4	3
4	3	1	5	2	6
3	4	5	2	6	1
6	1	2	4	3	5
5	6	4	3	1	2
1	2	3	6	5	4

b)

1	3	5	2	6	4
2	4	6	3	5	1
3	6	4	5	1	2
5	1	2	6	4	3
6	2	1	4	3	5
4	5	3	1	2	6

TRAVEL PUZZLE 49

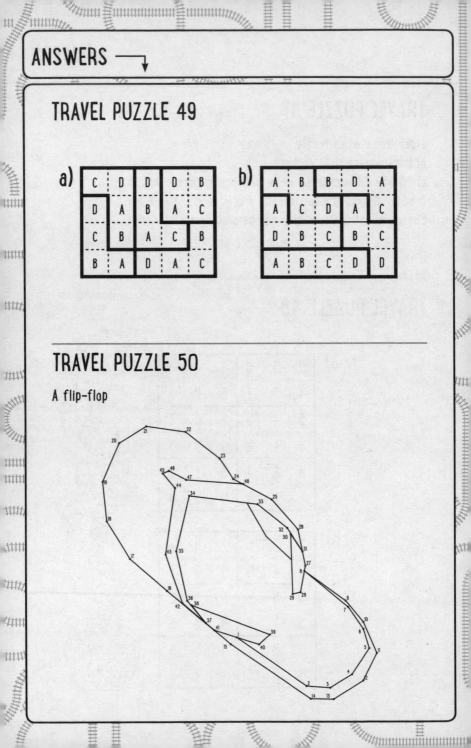

a)

C	D	D	D	B
D	A	B	A	C
C	B	A	C	B
B	A	D	A	C

b)

A	B	B	D	A
A	C	D	A	C
D	B	C	B	C
A	B	C	D	D

TRAVEL PUZZLE 50

A flip-flop

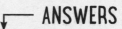

TRAVEL PUZZLE 51

Algeria: 4 (Africa)
Argentina: 7 (South America)
Australia: 1 (Oceania)
Brazil: 7 (South America)
Canada: 6 (North America)
China: 3 (Asia)
France: 5 (Europe)
Germany: 5 (Europe)
India: 3 (Asia)

Italy: 5 (Europe)
Japan: 3 (Asia)
Mexico: 6 (North America)
Morocco: 4 (Africa)
New Zealand: 1 (Oceania)
South Korea: 3 (Asia)
Switzerland: 5 (Europe)
United Kingdom: 5 (Europe)
United States: 6 (North America)

TRAVEL PUZZLE 52

a) CAR
b) BOAT
c) TAXI
d) PLANE
e) HELICOPTER

TRAVEL PUZZLE 53

TRAVEL PUZZLE 54

a)

b)

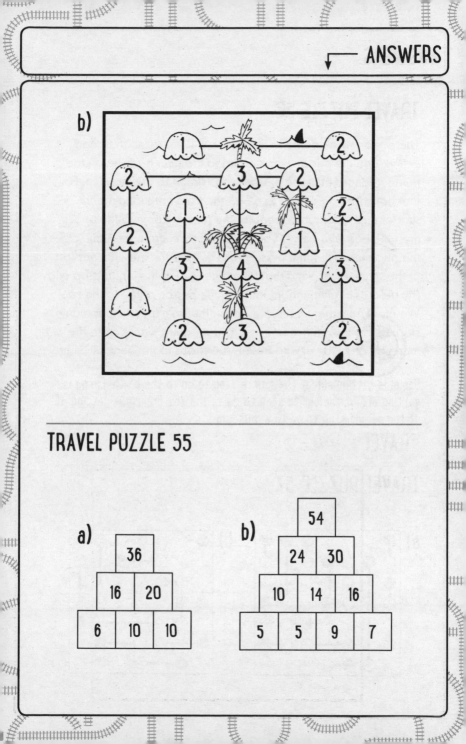

TRAVEL PUZZLE 55

a)

```
      36
   16    20
  6   10   10
```

b)

```
         54
      24    30
    10   14   16
   5    5    9    7
```

TRAVEL PUZZLE 56

The person who's going to the beach will get off sooner than Emma, and the person who's going to the beach will be on the train for longer than the person who's going to the museum. For that beach-going person to be on the train both longer and shorter times than other people, the person going to the beach must the one who gets off at the fourth stop. From the same clues this also means that the person who goes to the museum gets off at the second stop, and that Emma gets off at the eighth stop and (by process of elimination) must be the person going to the zoo. We also know that Daniel will be on the train for twice as many stops as Francis, so it must Francis who travels two stops to the museum, and Daniel who travels four stops to the beach.

Daniel is getting off at the fourth stop to go to the beach. Emma is getting off at the eighth stop to go to the zoo. Francis is getting off at the second stop to go to a museum.

TRAVEL PUZZLE 57

a)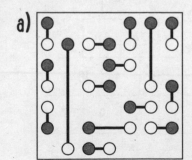

b)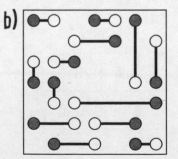

TRAVEL PUZZLE 58

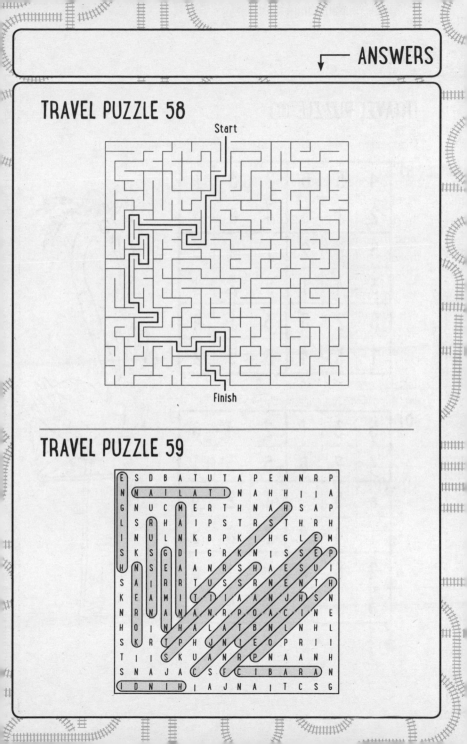

TRAVEL PUZZLE 59

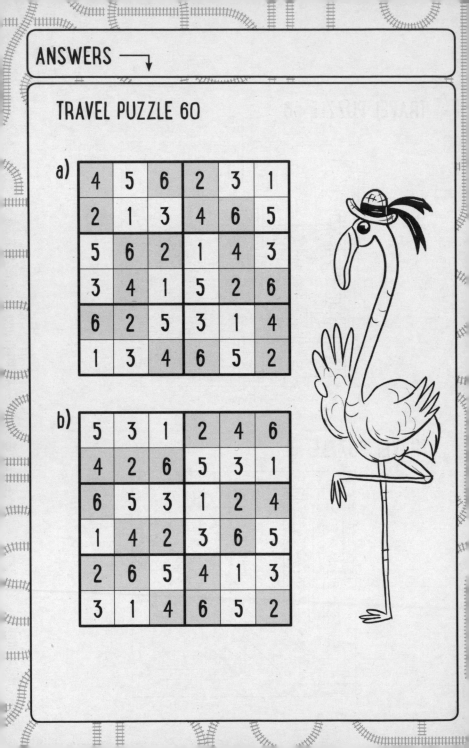

TRAVEL PUZZLE 60

a)

4	5	6	2	3	1
2	1	3	4	6	5
5	6	2	1	4	3
3	4	1	5	2	6
6	2	5	3	1	4
1	3	4	6	5	2

b)

5	3	1	2	4	6
4	2	6	5	3	1
6	5	3	1	2	4
1	4	2	3	6	5
2	6	5	4	1	3
3	1	4	6	5	2

TRAVEL PUZZLE 61

TRAVEL PUZZLE 62

The lowest point on Earth that's still dry land is the shore of the Dead Sea, which is about 420 m (1,375 ft) below sea level.

TRAVEL PUZZLE 63

a) 6
b) 15
c) 18

TRAVEL PUZZLE 64

Cube c is the correct one. The ice cream is facing the wrong way on cube a. On cube b there would be a flower on top if the ball and star faced forward, and the ball and star would be facing different ways, too. On cube d there should be a ball on top, not a wheel.

TRAVEL PUZZLE 65

a)

1	6	2	3	4	5
2	1	4	5	3	6
4	5	6	2	1	3
3	2	1	6	5	4
6	3	5	4	2	1
5	4	3	1	6	2

b)

1	4	3	5	6	2
5	1	6	2	3	4
6	2	5	4	1	3
3	5	2	1	4	6
2	3	4	6	5	1
4	6	1	3	2	5

TRAVEL PUZZLE 66

1) ANT
2) NEAT
3) AGENT
4) MAGNET
5) MAGENTA

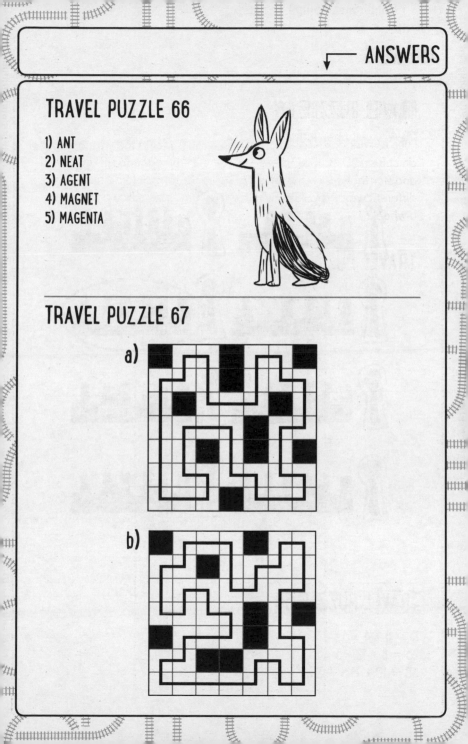

TRAVEL PUZZLE 67

a)

b)

TRAVEL PUZZLE 68

The key will open lock d.

TRAVEL PUZZLE 69

15 = 8 + 4 + 3
23 = 8 + 12 + 3
30 = 10 + 13 + 7

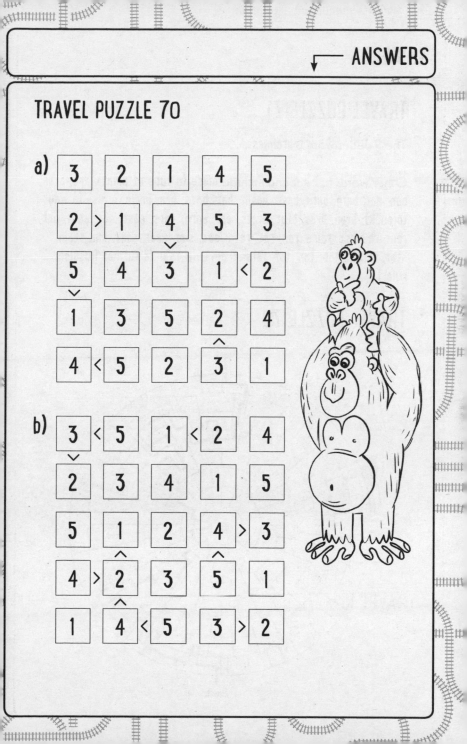

TRAVEL PUZZLE 70

a)

3	2	1	4	5
2 > 1	4	5	3
5	4	3	1 < 2
1	3	5	2	4
4 < 5	2	3	1

b)

3 < 5	1 < 2	4
2	3	4	1	5
5	1	2	4 > 3
4 > 2	3	5	1
1	4 < 5	3 > 2

TRAVEL PUZZLE 71

The 9-letter word is **brainiest**.

Other words to be found include anise (a type of plant), art, arts, ban, bar, barn, bars, base, basin, bat, bats, bra, brain, braise (a way to cook), bran, bras, brat, brats, ear, earn, ears, east, eat, eats, nab, rain, rainiest, raise, ran, rat, rats, sat, sea, sear, seat, sin, stain, star, strain, tab, tan, tar, tars, train and tsar (a former Russian ruler).

TRAVEL PUZZLE 72

Start

Finish

TRAVEL PUZZLE 73

An apple costs **4 cents**, an orange costs **3 cents** and a pineapple costs **8 cents**.

TRAVEL PUZZLE 74

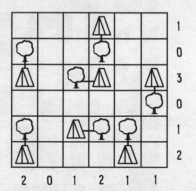

TRAVEL PUZZLE 75

The Dyson family have more children than the family in lane 1, which means that, because no lane number matches the number of children in a car, they are in lane 2 with 3 children in the car, or are in lane 3 with 2 children in the car. However, we also know that they have an odd number of children in the car, so therefore they must be in lane 2 with 3 children in the car. This also means that (again, because no lane number matches the number of children in a car) that the car with 1 child in must be in lane 3, and so the car with 2 children in must be in lane 1. We are told that the Walker family are in a lower-numbered lane than the car with 1 child, so they must be the car in lane 1, and the remaining family (the Briscoes) must be in lane 3.

The Briscoe family are in lane 3 and have one child. The Dyson family are in lane 2 and have three children. The Walker family are in lane 1 and have two children.

TRAVEL PUZZLE 76

Note that you could place **IRAN** or **IRAQ** in either space.

TRAVEL PUZZLE 77

a)

	3	6			3	7
4	1	3		6 / 9	2	4
3	2	1	9 / 20	5	1	3
	14	2	9	3	7	
	4	7 / 11	8	1	2	13
6	1	2	3	5	1	4
8	3	5		13	4	9

b)

			5	6		
		3 / 13	2	1		
	6 / 4	1	3	2	14	3
4	1	3	14 / 6	3	9	2
14	3	9	2	3 / 3	2	1
		6	1	2	3	
		4	3	1		

TRAVEL PUZZLE 78

a)

3	2	19	20	25
4	1	18	21	24
5	6	17	22	23
8	7	16	15	14
9	10	11	12	13

b)

21	20	5	4	3
22	19	6	7	2
23	18	17	8	1
24	15	16	9	10
25	14	13	12	11

TRAVEL PUZZLE 79

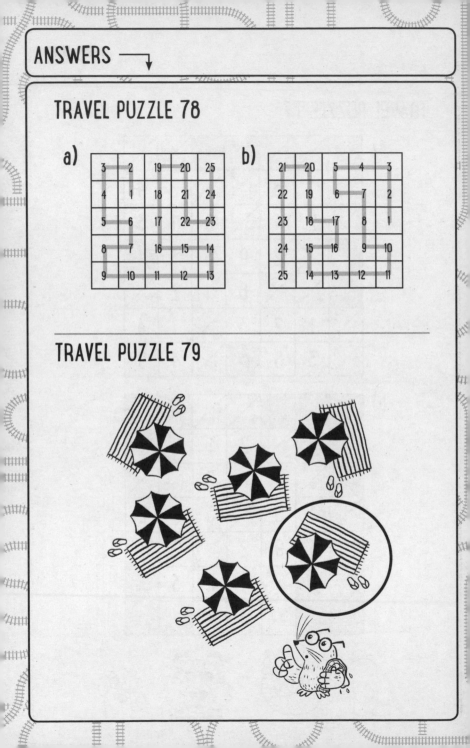

TRAVEL PUZZLE 80

a)

2	3	6	4	1	5
4	1	5	2	3	6
3	6	4	1	5	2
1	5	2	3	6	4
6	4	1	5	2	3
5	2	3	6	4	1

b)

2	1	4	6	3	5
3	5	2	1	4	6
4	6	3	5	2	1
5	2	1	4	6	3
1	4	6	3	5	2
6	3	5	2	1	4

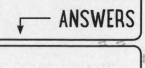

TRAVEL PUZZLE 81

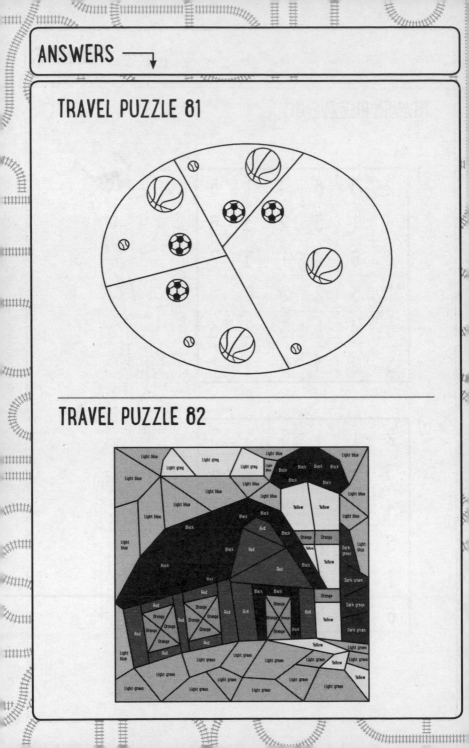

TRAVEL PUZZLE 82

TRAVEL PUZZLE 83

TRAVEL PUZZLE 84

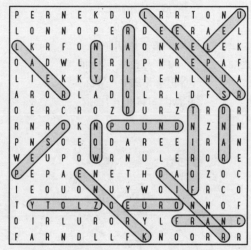

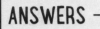

TRAVEL PUZZLE 85

Australia – Dollar
Brazil – Real
China – Yuan
Denmark – Krone
Egypt – Pound
France – Euro
Hungary – Forint

India – Rupee
Mexico – Peso
Russia – Rouble
South Africa – Rand
South Korea – Won
Switzerland – Franc

TRAVEL PUZZLE 86

a)

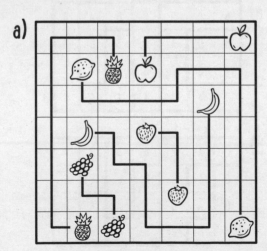

b)

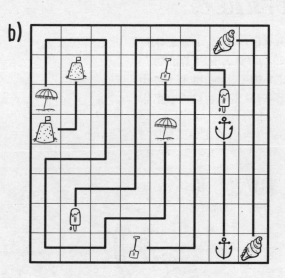

TRAVEL PUZZLE 87

There are **48 cubes**: 8 cubes on the top layer, 10 cubes on the second layer down, 14 cubes on the third layer down and 16 cubes on the bottom layer.

TRAVEL PUZZLE 88

The 7-letter word is **bounced**.

Other words to be found include **bode, bond, bone, bounce, bound, cob, cod, code, con, cone, doc, doe, don, done, duo, eon, nod, node, ode, once, one, ounce** and **undo**.

TRAVEL PUZZLE 89

17 = 7 + 10 (burst 12, 8, 11 and 4)
20 = 8 + 12 (burst 7, 11, 4 and 10)
32 = 4 + 7 + 10 + 11 (burst 12 and 8)
38 = 7 + 8 + 11 + 12 (burst 4 and 10)

TRAVEL PUZZLE 90

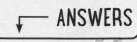

ANSWERS

TRAVEL PUZZLE 91

a)

6	5	1	3	4	2
2	1	5	4	6	3
3	2	6	1	5	4
4	3	2	6	1	5
5	6	4	2	3	1
1	4	3	5	2	6

b)

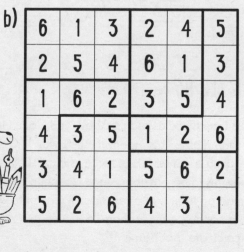

6	1	3	2	4	5
2	5	4	6	1	3
1	6	2	3	5	4
4	3	5	1	2	6
3	4	1	5	6	2
5	2	6	4	3	1

TRAVEL PUZZLE 92

Start

Finish

TRAVEL PUZZLE 93

Conchita is less than twice as old as Abby, and Conchita is also 7 years older than Abby. This means if Abby was 1, Conchita would be 8 – which is not less than twice as old. Abby needs to be at least 8 for this to be possible, since Conchita would then be 15. And this must be their two ages, since if Conchita was any older she would not be younger than 16. Given that Abby is 8, you can then calculate that Ben is 12.

So Abby is 8, Ben is 12 and Conchita is 15.

TRAVEL PUZZLE 94

a)

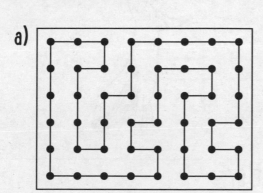

b)

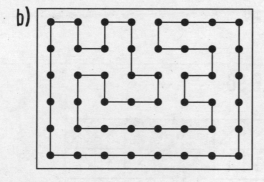

TRAVEL PUZZLE 95

Shape 4 because it is the only concave shape. A shape is concave if it has an inwards 'dent', or in other words if it has an internal angle that is greater than 180 degrees.

TRAVEL PUZZLE 96

1) SEE
2) SEED
3) REEDS
4) ERASED
5) GREASED
6) DISAGREE

TRAVEL PUZZLE 97

1) 8pm
2) 7pm the previous day

TRAVEL PUZZLE 98

a)

	11	6				4	3
4	3	1			4 / 16	3	1
10	8	2	11	12 / 8	9	1	2
	11	3	5	1	2		
		7	1	2	4	14	
	17	11 / 3	3	5	1	2	3
11	8	1	2		11	9	2
11	9	2			4	3	1

b)

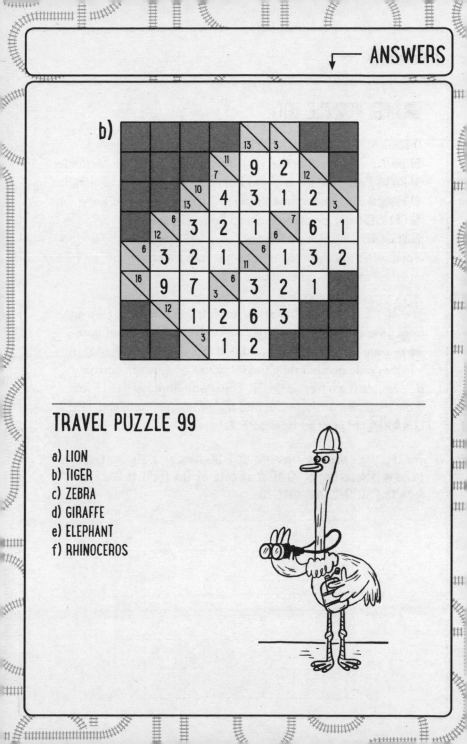

The grid contains the following entries (kakuro-style puzzle):

			13 \	3 \		
	11 \ 7	9	2	12 \		
	10 \ 13	4	3	1	2	3 \
6 \ 12	3	2	1	7 \ 6	6	1
6 \	3	2	1	6 \ 11| 1	3	2
16 \	9	7	6 \ 3	3	2	1
	12 \	1	2	6	3	
		3 \	1	2		

TRAVEL PUZZLE 99

a) LION
b) TIGER
c) ZEBRA
d) GIRAFFE
e) ELEPHANT
f) RHINOCEROS

TRAVEL PUZZLE 100

The 10:40 flight has a higher gate number than the flight to Rome, so we know that the 10:40 flight is not the flight to Rome. We also know that the flight to Rome (which is not at 10:40) has a higher gate number than the 11:00 flight, so we also know that the 11:00 flight is not the flight to Rome. So the flight to Rome must be 10:15, since it's the only time left. The flight to London leaves after the flight to Paris, so the Paris flight must be 10.40 and the London flight must be 11:00.

The 10:15 flight, which we now know is to Rome, is not leaving from gate 20, so the Rome flight must leave from either gate 26 or gate 31. We are also told that the 10:40 Paris flight has a higher gate number than the flight to Rome, which can only be possible if it is from gate 31. This means that the 10:15 Rome flight must be from gate 26, and therefore the remaining 11:00 London flight must be from gate 20.

The flight to London is departing at 11:00 from gate 20. The flight to Paris is departing at 10:40 from gate 31. The flight to Rome is departing at 10:15 from gate 26.

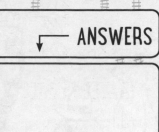

TRAVEL PUZZLE 101

THE END.
WELL
DONE!

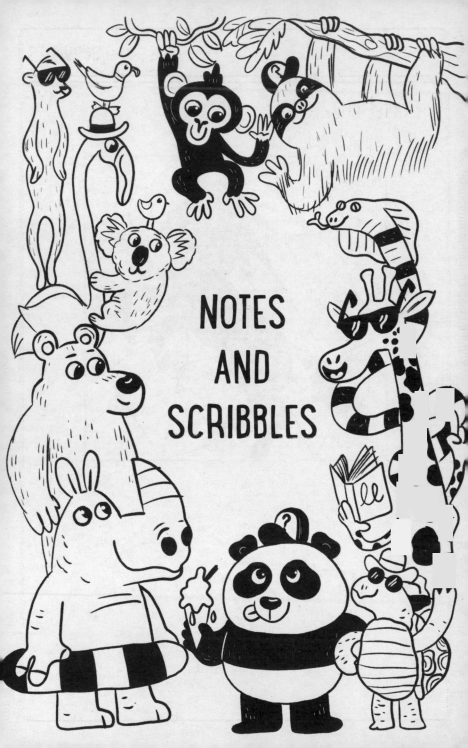

NOTES

AND

SCRIBBLES

NOTES AND SCRIBBLES →

NOTES AND SCRIBBLES →

NOTES AND SCRIBBLES ⟶

ALSO AVAILABLE:

ISBN 9781780556659

ISBN 9781780556642

ISBN 9781780556192

ISBN 9781780553085

ISBN 9781780556185

ISBN 9781780555935

ISBN 9781780555621

ISBN 9781780556635

ISBN 9781780554730

ISBN 9781780554723

ISBN 9781780555409

ISBN 9781780556208

ISBN 9781780553146

ISBN 9781780553078

ISBN 9781780556628

ISBN 9781780552491